Cauldron & Candlelight: Celebrations of the Wheel

Sabbat Recipes, Invocations, and Blessings for Every Season

by Morgelyn Hearthwood

Ember & Ink Books

Copyright © 2025 by Morgelyn Hearthwood
All rights reserved.

No part of this publication may be reproduced, distributed, or transmitted in any form or by any means, including photocopying, recording, or other electronic or mechanical methods, without the prior written permission of the author, except in the case of brief quotations embodied in critical reviews and certain other noncommercial uses permitted by copyright law.

For permission requests, contact the author at:
morgelynhearthwood@gmail.com

This book is a work of original authorship. All recipes, invocations, and blessings are the intellectual property of the author. Any resemblance to traditional texts or practices is purely coincidental or respectfully adapted with credit to cultural roots.

Published by Ember & Ink Books
Second Edition: 2025
ISBN: 978-1-7641293-0-5
Cover and interior design by the author.
Illustrations by Morgelyn Hearthwood

Dedicated to Tracy and Rikki, and to Mandy and Pat —

whose hearths have offered warmth, laughter, and cherished company through many happy hours.

Introduction

Welcome to Cauldron & Candlelight: Celebrations of the Wheel. This book is a heartfelt collection of recipes, invocations, and blessings designed to honor and celebrate the seasons of the Wheel of the Year. Whether you're new to the Wheel or a seasoned practitioner, I hope this guide adds a touch of warmth and magic to your celebrations.

The Wheel of the Year is a beautiful way to connect with the rhythms of nature. Each turn of the wheel marks a moment of growth, rest, and transformation. Through these pages, you will find recipes to nourish both body and spirit, invocations to invoke the energy of the Sabbats, and blessings to offer gratitude to the cycles of life.

This book is a celebration of the Earth's bounty, of cooking with intention, and of the magic that comes from sharing meals with loved ones. From the hearty feasts of Winter Solstice to the bright, fresh flavors of Beltane, each recipe reflects the essence of the season it honors. The blessings and invocations are designed to align you with the energy of the Sabbats, to deepen your connection with nature's rhythms.

I invite you to use this book as a guide to bringing more magic into your kitchen and your home, to help you celebrate the changing seasons with love and intention. Whether you're preparing a special meal for yourself or gathering with friends and family, may each recipe, blessing, and invocation nourish your body, soul, and spirit.

Blessed be.
Morgelyn Hearthwood

Table of Contents

Title Page I

Copyright II

Dedication... III

Introduction IV

Table of Contents .... V-XII

Yule

Yule Title Page 1
Yule Introduction 2
Invocation 3
Blessing 4

Recipes

- Apple Cinnamon Solstice Scroll.. 5
- Cranberry & Orange Biscotti... 6
- Cranberry & Orange Loaf.. 7
- Gingerbread Cake.. 8.
- Spelt & Herb Yule Rolls.. 9
- Yule Log Cake... 10
- Buttered Cabbage with Toasted Caraway...................... 11
- Chestnut & Mushroom Pithivier..................................... 12
- Glazed Roast Loin of Pork with Apple............................ 13
- Hearty Winter Solstice Stew... 14
- Herb & Chestnut Stuffing Bake....................................... 15
- Herbed Winter Solstice Pie... 16
- Honey-glazed Roast Root Veggies.................................. 17
- Slow Cooker Solstice Roast... 18
- Winter Root Veg and Barley Bake................................... 19
- Gingerbread Trifle.. 20
- Honey & Cardamom Baked Pears.................................. 21
- Peppermint Bark Brownie Bites...................................... 22
- Peppermint Bark.. 23
- Snowflake Sugar Cookies.. 24
- Spiced Apple Crumble Bar.. 25
- Spiced Solstice Shortbread... 26
- Yule Spiced Cookies... 27
- Chocolate Peppermint Elixir... 28
- Mulled Mead.. 29
- Spiced Cranberry Punch... 30

Table of Contents
Yule contd.

- Winter Solstice Wassail..................................31
- Yule Herbal Chai..32
- Caramelized Onion Cranberry Relish............33
- Solstice Herbed Salt Blend..........................34
- 35

Imbolc

Imbolc Title Page 37
Imbolc Introduction 38
Invocation 39
Blessing 40

Recipes

- Brigid's Braided Bread..................................41
- Honeyed Oat Cakes.....................................42
- Milk & Herb Bread Rolls...............................43
- Cinnamon Apple Braided Bread....................44
- Herbed Cheese & Seed Crackers..................45
- Oat & Honey Bannocks................................46
- Sun Wheel Scones......................................47
- Cauliflower & White Bean Gratin..................48
- Brigid's Flame Pie.......................................49
- Candlemas Cheese & Herb Tartlets..............50
- Fire Roasted Red Pepper & Goat Cheese Galette.........51
- Imbolc Shepherd's Bake with Lentils & Roots...............52
- Brigid's Hearth Baked Rice Pudding..............53
- Honey & Oat Brittle....................................54
- Imbolc Milk Pudding with Spiced Pears.........55
- Spiced Custard Tarts..................................56
- White Chocolate & Lavender Bark................57
- Brigid's Blessing Milk Tea............................58
- Creamy Vanilla Oat Nog..............................59
- Golden Oat Moon Milk................................60
- Mulled White Wine.....................................61
- Lemon & Honey Hearth Tea........................62
- Fairy Lavender Wine...................................63
- Citrus & Chamomile Marmalade...................64
- Honey Butter Spread..................................65
- Lemon and Thyme Jelly..............................66
- Milk & Rose Petal Jam.................................67
- Vanilla Pear Preserve..................................68
- 69

Table of Contents

Ostara

Ostara Title Page 71
Ostara Introduction 72
Invocation 73
Blessing 74

Recipes

- Bird's Nest Macaroons.. 75
- Carrot & Honey Mini Loaves... 76
- Blossom Muffins... 77
- Egg Bread Nests.. 78
- Seed Cake... 79
- Spring Herb Scones... 80
- Spring Onion & Feta Flatbreads... 81
- Bacon & Spring Onion Quiche... 82
- Chickpea & Lemon Skillet Stew... 83
- Devilled Eggs with Spring Herbs & Flowers........................... 84
- Herbed Spring Lamb Chops... 85
- Honey Mustard Glazed Chicken with Spring Vegetables....... 86
- Herb & Ricotta Tart... 87
- Pickled Quail Eggs... 88
- Rabbit & Root Vegetable Pie... 89
- Smoked Fish & Herb Cakes.. 90
- Spring Green Frittata.. 91
- Spring Pea & Mint Dip... 92
- Stuffed Portobello Mushrooms with Barley & Herbs............ 93
- Wild Garlic & Potato Cakes... 94
- Honey & Chamomile Custards... 95
- Honey-Ricotta Stuffed Dates with Pistachio Crumble........... 96
- Lemon Curd Tartlets... 97
- Carrot Truffles.. 98
- Fruit Leathers... 99
- Sheep Shaped Honey Cookies... 100
- Sugared Candies Nuts... 101
- Blossom Tea Blend.. 102
- Blossom Sugar Cubes.. 103
- Wild Garlic & Lemon Butter.. 104
- 105

Table of Contents

Beltane

- Beltane Title Page 107
  - Beltane Introduction 108
  - Invocation 109
  - Blessing 110

Recipes

- Asparagus Puff Pastry Twists..........................111
- Traditional Bannock..112
- Lemon Balm Scones with Honey Butter..........113
- Wild Garlic and Herb Bread............................114
- Floral Goat Cheese Dip with Edible Blossoms..115
- Grilled Haloumi Skewers................................116
- Honey Glazed Roast Veggie Tart....................117
- Lamb and Rosemary Pies...............................118
- New Potato and Chive Salad..........................119
- Roasted Beet and Orange Salad....................120
- Rosemary Honey Chicken with edible flowers..121
- Spiced Root Veg Fritters................................122
- Spring Greens Salad with edible Flowers......123
- Spring Vegetable Risotto...............................124
- Stuffed Portobello Mushrooms......................125
- Elderflower Jelly with Wild Berries................126
- Honey Rose Shortbread.................................127
- Maypole Parfait Cups....................................128
- Rhubarb and Vanilla Crumble.......................129
- Strawberries and Cream Fairy Cakes............130
- Beltane Blossom Fizz....................................131
- Hawthorn Cordial..132
- Meadow Mead Spritz....................................133
- Strawberry Mint Beltane Cooler...................134
- Beltane Fire Butter.......................................135
- Dandelion Jelly...136
- 137

Table of Contents
Litha

Litha Title Page 139
Litha Introduction 140
Invocation 141
Blessing 142

Recipes

- Sun Wheel Braided Bread..143
- Honey Oat Harvest Loaf..144
- Lemon Verbena Shortbread Cookies..............................145
- Herb & Flower Focaccia...146
- Rosemary & Olive Sun Bread..147
- Golden Litha Honey Cake..148
- Grilled Vegetable Skewers...149
- Herbed Goat Cheese & Edible Flower Crostini..............150
- Lemon Balm Chicken Thighs...151
- Herb-Crusted Salmon with Citrus Butter......................152
- Mini Spinach & Fetta Pastry Twists...............................153
- Peach & Honey Midsummer Galette..............................154
- Savoury Summer Herb & Cheese Hand Pies.................155
- Stuffed Zucchini Boats..156
- Summer Garden Pasta with Roasted Cherry Tomatoes..157
- Summer Solstice Corn Fritters with Spiced Aioli..........158
- Sunshine Stuffed Bell Peppers with Couscous & Summer Veggies..159
- Caramelized Peach and Thyme Tartlets........................160
- Watermelon Fetta & Mint Skewers................................161
- Chilled Honeyed Cherry Fool..162
- Midsummer Berry Crumble Bars....................................163
- Lemon Balm & Lavender Sun Tea..................................164
- Vanilla Rose Moon Milk...165
- Peach & Thyme Solstice spritz.......................................166
- Sun-Kissed Berry Citrus Punch.......................................167
- Quick-Pickled Cucumber & Radish.................................168
- Strawberry-Rose Preserve...169
- Thyme Simple Syrup..170
- 171

Table of Contents
Lammas / Lughnasadh

Lammas Title Page 173
Lammas Introduction 174
Invocation 175
Blessing 176

Recipes

- Golden Sunflower Bread... 177
- Seed Crackers... 178
- Rustic Barley Bread... 179
- Sundried Tomato & Basil Bread...................................... 180
- Caramelized Onion & Goat Cheese Tartlets................... 181
- Cornbread with Fresh Herbs.. 182
- Fresh Tomato Tart.. 183
- Garlic & Herb White Bean Dip.. 184
- Grilled Eggplant with Garlic & Mint................................ 185
- Herb-Marinated Chicken Skewars.................................. 186
- Peach & Cream Cheese Pastries..................................... 187
- Roasted Vegetable Galette... 188
- Rosemary Roasted Potato Wedges................................ 189
- Summer Squash Casserole... 190
- Sweet Corn & Honey Fritters... 191
- Zucchini & Sweet Corn Fritters...................................... 192
- Golden Honeycomb Candy... 193
- Honey & Almond Shortbread... 194
- Honey & Lavender Ice Cream... 195
- Lemon Balm Tea Cakes... 196
- Strawberry Lammas Bars.. 197
- Golden Honey Mead Spritzer... 198
- Herbal Lemonade for Lammas....................................... 199
- Sweet Corn Silk Tea.. 200
- Blueberry & Lavender Jam... 201
- Herbed Butter for Bread Blessing.................................. 202
- Peach & Thyme Chutney... 203
- Roasted Tomato & Garlic Relish..................................... 204
- 205

Table of Contents
Mabon

- Mabon Title Page 207
- Mabon Introduction 208
- Invocation 209
- Blessing 210

Recipes

- Cranberry Walnut Bread 211
- Cheddar & Chive Oat Biscuit 212
- Fig & Hazelnut Honey Cake 213
- Pumpkin & Sage Scones 214
- Spiced Apple & Walnut Muffins 215
- Bacon Wrapped Stuffed Chicken Breasts 216
- Beef & Ale Pie with Herby Crust 217
- Harvest Galette 218
- Stuffed Acorn Squash 219
- Maple Pecan Baked Brie 220
- Mushrooms & Chestnut Pot Pie 221
- Pork & Apple Harvest Skillet 222
- Pumpkin & Sage Hand Pies 223
- Blackberry & Apple Crumble 224
- Roasted Root Veggie Medley 225
- Caramel Apple Hand Pies 226
- Chai-Spiced Rice Pudding 227
- Pear & Thyme Crumble 228
- Spiced Pear & Honey Tart 229
- Chai-Spiced Hot Chocolate 230
- Elderberry & Hibiscus Fizz 231
- Mulled Blackberry & Apple Cider 232
- Rosemary Pear Sparkle 233
- Spiced Apple Cider 234
- Spiced Pumpkin Smoothie 235
- Berry & Lavender Jam 236
- Pear & Ginger Jam 237
- Pickled Red Onions with Thyme 238
- Pumpkin Chutney 239
- Spiced Apple Butter 240
- 241

Table of Contents
Samhain

Samhain Title Page 243
Samhain Introduction 244
Invocation 245
Blessing 246

Recipes

- Blood Orange & Clove Muffins........................... 247
- Cider-Glazed Apple Bread.................................. 248
- Cinnamon Hazelnut Bread................................. 249
- Midnight Ash Cake... 250
- Shadow Moon Cookies...................................... 251
- Spiced Soul Cakes.. 252
- Black Garlic & Mushroom Pie............................. 253
- Dark Ale & Onion Sausages................................ 254
- Roast Pumpkin & Chestnut Bake........................ 255
- Root & Barley Stew.. 256
- Shepherd's Pie... 257
- Amber Sugar Skulls... 258
- Ancestor's Baked Apples.................................... 259
- Candied Rosemary Pears.................................... 260
- Soulfire Fudge.. 261
- Spirit-Walk Truffles... 262
- Witchlight Treacle Tart....................................... 263
- Ancestor's Mulberry Cordial............................... 264
- Blackberry & Elder Syrup.................................... 265
- Blood Moon Beetroot Latte............................... 266
- Ghost Milk Moon Elixir....................................... 267
- Mulled Blackberry Wine..................................... 268
- Witch's Bonfire Cider... 269
- Caramelised Onion & Fig Relish.......................... 270
- Cranberry & Orange Spirit Jam........................... 271
- Mulling Spice Sachets... 272
- Smokey Beet & Apple Chutney........................... 273
- Spiced Pumpkin Butter....................................... 274
- 275

Yule: A Feast of Light in the Dark

As the wheel turns and winter deepens, we arrive at Yule, the Winter Solstice—the longest night and the rebirth of the Sun. Celebrated around December 21st in the Northern Hemisphere, this ancient Sabbat marks the point when darkness begins to give way to light once more. Cultures across time, from Norse to Celtic, have honored this pivotal turning with rituals, firelight, and feasting.

Yule is a time of stillness, reflection, and hope—a sacred pause in the heart of winter. For our ancestors, it was both a spiritual and practical celebration. The returning sun meant the promise of spring, but food was still scarce. Every ingredient was precious, and the hearth became the heart of midwinter magic.

In Norse tradition, the Yule log burned through the night to protect the household and encourage the sun's return. Evergreen boughs, holly, and mistletoe symbolized life that endures. Feasts were shared to honor the gods, the spirits of the land, and the bonds of kin.

Today, we continue these traditions by gathering loved ones, kindling candles or fires, and preparing special foods that nourish the body and spirit. Spices warm us from within, evergreen herbs connect us to ancient wisdom, and every dish becomes a blessing.

These Yule recipes are crafted with heart, echoing the themes of rebirth, generosity, and light in the darkness. Whether you're feasting alone or with a circle of loved ones, may your table be full, your home warm, and your spirit lifted.

Yule Invocation

By flame and frost, by moon and sun,
The longest night has now begun.
Yet in this dark, the light is born—
A spark of gold on Solstice morn.
Spirits of hearth, of root and flame,
We call you here in Yule's bright name.
Bless these hands, this food, this fire,
With joy, with peace, with heart's desire.
Let cinnamon, clove, and honeyed bread
Be offerings to those who've led.
Let laughter rise, and cups be raised
In honor of the light reclaimed.
With holly crowned and candles bright,
We cook, we stir, we share the night.
By every spell and sacred rite,
May warmth and love our hearts ignite.
So be it now, and ever true—
Blessed be this Feast of Yule.

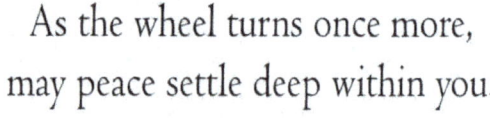

Yule Blessing

May the light of the reborn sun
shine gently upon your path.
May your hearth be warm,
your table full,
and your heart alight with joy.

May spices stir memories,
and sweetness awaken hope.
May each shared dish be a spell—
of comfort, connection, and care.

As the wheel turns once more,
may peace settle deep within you.
May love gather round you
like evergreens in winter.

And may the magic of Yule
bless your home with renewal,
your hands with purpose,
and your spirit with light.

So may it be.

Apple Cinnamon Solstice Scrolls

Ingredients
(Makes 12 scrolls)

- 3 cups plain flour
- 2¼ tsp (1 packet) instant yeast
- ¼ cup sugar
- ½ tsp salt
- ¾ cup warm milk
- ¼ cup melted butter
- 1 egg
- Filling:
  o 2 apples, peeled and finely chopped
  o ¼ cup brown sugar
  o 1 tbsp cinnamon
  o 1 tbsp melted butter

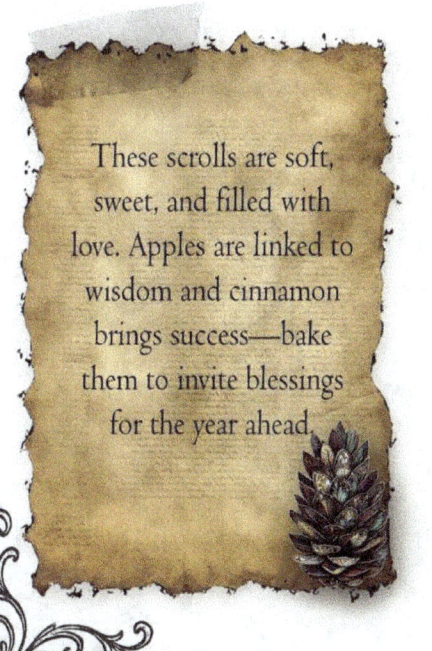

These scrolls are soft, sweet, and filled with love. Apples are linked to wisdom and cinnamon brings success—bake them to invite blessings for the year ahead.

Method

1. Combine flour, yeast, sugar, and salt. Mix in warm milk, melted butter, and egg.
2. Knead until smooth (about 8 minutes), then cover and let rise 1 hour.
3. Roll dough into a rectangle. Brush with melted butter and sprinkle with apples, sugar, and cinnamon.
4. Roll up and slice into 12 pieces.
5. Place in a greased dish, cover, and rise 30 mins.
6. Bake at 180°C (350°F) for 25–30 minutes.

Cranberry & Orange Biscotti

Ingredients
(Makes about 24)

- 2¼ cups plain flour
- 1½ tsp baking powder
- ¾ cup sugar
- Zest of 1 orange
- 3 eggs
- ¾ cup dried cranberries
- Optional: ½ cup chopped almonds

Method

1. Preheat oven to 160°C (320°F). Line a tray.
2. Mix flour, baking powder, sugar, and zest. Beat in eggs to form dough.
3. Stir in cranberries (and almonds if using).
4. Shape into 2 logs. Bake 25 minutes. Cool slightly.
5. Slice diagonally and bake slices another 10–15 mins until crisp.

These crunchy, zesty treats are perfect for dunking in Yule tea or gifting with a ribbon and a charm.

Cranberry Orange Loaf

Ingredients
(Makes 1 loaf)

- 2 cups plain flour
- 1½ tsp baking powder
- ½ tsp salt
- ½ cup butter, softened
- ¾ cup sugar
- 2 eggs
- Zest of 1 orange
- ½ cup orange juice
- 1½ cups fresh or dried cranberries

Bright and tangy, this loaf brings a splash of colour to the darkest days. Cranberries are protective and oranges attract joy—making this a powerful solstice treat.

Method

1. Preheat oven to 175°C (350°F). Grease and line a loaf tin.
2. Mix flour, baking powder, and salt.
3. In another bowl, cream butter and sugar. Add eggs one at a time. Stir in orange zest and juice.
4. Gently fold in dry ingredients, then add cranberries.
5. Pour into tin and bake 50–60 minutes, until a skewer comes out clean.
6. Cool before slicing.

Gingerbread Cake
with Lemon Glaze

Ingredients
(Serves 8)

- 1½ cups plain flour
- 1 tsp baking soda
- 2 tsp ground ginger
- 1 tsp cinnamon
- ½ tsp ground cloves
- ¼ tsp salt
- ½ cup brown sugar
- ½ cup molasses
- ½ cup unsalted butter, melted
- 1 egg
- ½ cup hot water

Lemon Glaze:
- ½ cup icing sugar
- 2 tsp lemon juice
- Zest of ½ lemon

Method

1. Preheat oven to 175°C (350°F). Grease a small cake tin.
2. Mix flour, baking soda, spices, and salt in a bowl.
3. In another bowl, combine sugar, molasses, butter, and egg. Add dry ingredients gradually, then mix in hot water.
4. Pour into tin and bake 35–40 minutes. Cool.
5. Mix glaze ingredients and drizzle over cooled cake.

A spicy, warming treat with a touch of brightness from the lemon—ideal after a hearty Yule meal.

Spelt & Herb Yule Rolls

Ingredients
(Makes 12 small rolls)

- 3 cups spelt flour
- 2 tsp instant yeast
- 1 tsp salt
- 1 tbsp dried herbs (e.g. marjoram, thyme, oregano)
- 1 tbsp olive oil
- 1 cup warm water

Method

1. Mix flour, yeast, salt, and herbs in a bowl. Add oil and water, stirring until dough forms.
2. Knead for 5–10 minutes until smooth. Cover and let rise 1 hour.
3. Divide into 12 balls, place on tray, and rest 20 minutes.
4. Bake at 200°C (390°F) for 15–20 minutes until golden.

These herb-infused rolls make a sacred offering—bake them with intention and share them with love.

Yule Log Cake
(Bûche de Noël)

Ingredients
(Serves 10–12)

For the sponge:
- 4 large eggs
- 100g (½ cup) caster sugar
- 1 tsp vanilla extract
- 65g (½ cup) plain flour
- 25g (¼ cup) cocoa powder
- ½ tsp baking powder
- Pinch of salt

For the filling:
- 200ml (¾ cup + 1 tbsp) double cream
- 2 tbsp icing sugar
- 1 tsp vanilla extract

For the ganache:
- 200g (7 oz) dark chocolate, chopped
- 200ml (¾ cup + 1 tbsp) double cream
- 1 tbsp butter

Method

1. Preheat oven to 180°C (350°F). Line a 23x33cm (9x13") Swiss roll tin with baking paper.
2. Beat eggs and sugar together until light and fluffy. Add vanilla.
3. Sift in flour, cocoa, baking powder, and salt. Gently fold until combined.
4. Pour into tin and bake 10–12 mins. Do not over-bake.
5. While warm, turn onto a tea towel dusted with icing sugar. Roll up sponge with towel and let cool.
6. For filling: whip cream, icing sugar, and vanilla to soft peaks. Unroll cake, spread filling, then re-roll.
7. For ganache: heat cream until just steaming, pour over chocolate. Let sit, then stir smooth. Add butter.
8. Spread ganache over cake. Use fork to make bark texture. Dust with icing sugar if desired.

Traditionally burned as a magical log, this sweet version honors the hearth and rebirth of the sun with chocolatey indulgence.

Buttered Cabbage
with Toasted Caraway

Ingredients
(Serves 4)

- ½ head green cabbage, thinly sliced
- 2 tbsp butter
- ½ tsp caraway seeds
- 1 tbsp apple cider vinegar
- Salt and pepper to taste

Cabbage carries old-world wisdom—paired with caraway, this dish brings protective energy and digestive ease.

Method

1. Melt butter in a large skillet. Add caraway seeds and toast until fragrant (about 30 seconds).
2. Add cabbage and sauté until just wilted and glossy (5–7 minutes).
3. Stir in vinegar, season to taste, and serve warm.

Chestnut and Mushroom Pithivier

Ingredients
(Serves 6)

- 2 sheets puff pastry
- 1 tbsp olive oil
- 1 onion, finely chopped
- 2 garlic cloves, minced
- 250g chestnut mushrooms, chopped
- 100g cooked chestnuts, chopped
- 1 tsp fresh thyme leaves
- Salt and pepper
- 1 egg, beaten (for brushing)

Method

1. Preheat oven to 200°C (400°F). Line a baking tray.
2. Heat oil in a pan. Sauté onion until soft, then add garlic, mushrooms, chestnuts, thyme, salt, and pepper. Cook until moisture evaporates. Cool.
3. Cut a large circle from one sheet of pastry and a slightly larger circle from the other.
4. Place filling in the center of the smaller circle, leaving a 2cm border.
5. Brush border with egg, place larger circle on top. Seal edges and crimp. Score a spiral pattern.
6. Brush with egg and bake for 30–35 minutes, until golden.

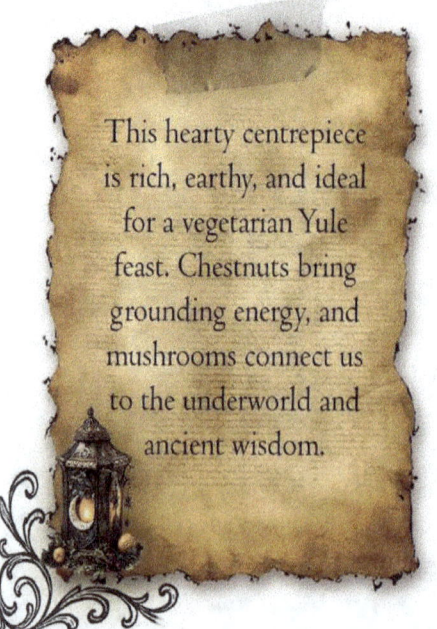

This hearty centrepiece is rich, earthy, and ideal for a vegetarian Yule feast. Chestnuts bring grounding energy, and mushrooms connect us to the underworld and ancient wisdom.

Glazed Roast Loin of Pork with Apples

Ingredients
(Serves 6–8)
- 1.5kg pork loin, scored
- Salt and pepper
- 2 tbsp olive oil
- 2 apples, quartered
- 1 onion, quartered
- Glaze:
  o 2 tbsp honey
  o 1 tbsp Dijon mustard
  o 1 tbsp apple cider vinegar

Method

1. Preheat oven to 190°C (375°F).
2. Rub pork with salt, pepper, and oil. Place in a roasting tin with apples and onion.
3. Mix glaze ingredients and brush over pork.
4. Roast for 1½ hours, basting occasionally, until golden and cooked through. Rest 10 minutes before carving.

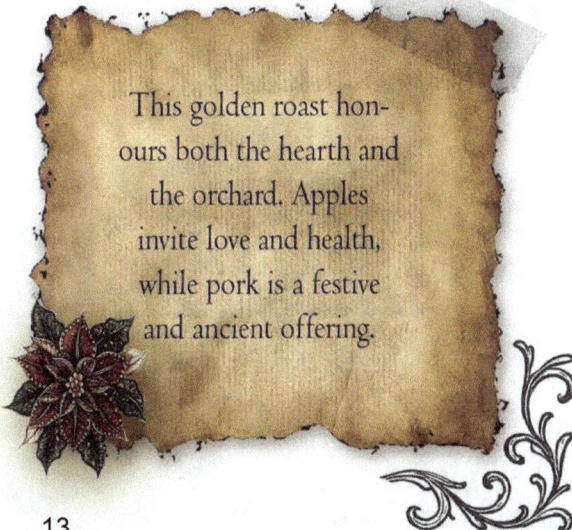

This golden roast honours both the hearth and the orchard. Apples invite love and health, while pork is a festive and ancient offering.

Hearty Winter Solstice Stew

Ingredients
(Serves 6)

- 2 tbsp olive oil
- 1 onion, chopped
- 2 garlic cloves, minced
- 2 carrots, chopped
- 2 parsnips, chopped
- 1 sweet potato, cubed
- 2 celery stalks, sliced
- 150g (¾ cup) dried green or brown lentils
- 1.5L (6 cups) vegetable broth
- 2 tsp dried thyme
- 1 tsp smoked paprika
- Salt and pepper, to taste
- Optional: kale or spinach, added at end

Method

1. Heat oil in large pot. Sauté onion and garlic until soft.
2. Add all veg and lentils. Stir in broth, herbs, paprika, salt and pepper.
3. Bring to boil, then reduce to simmer. Cover and cook 45–60 minutes.
4. Stir in leafy greens if using. Cook 5 more minutes. Adjust seasoning.

Packed with earth's bounty, this stew is a soul-soother. Stir clockwise for blessings!

Herb & Chestnut Stuffing Bake

Ingredients
(Serves 6–8)

- 200g roasted chestnuts, chopped
- 1 large onion, diced
- 2 celery stalks, diced
- 2 tbsp olive oil or butter
- 2 cloves garlic, minced
- 2 tbsp chopped fresh sage (or 2 tsp dried)
- 1 tbsp chopped fresh thyme
- 6 cups cubed day-old bread
- 2 cups vegetable or chicken stock
- Salt and pepper to taste

Method

1. Preheat oven to 180°C (350°F).
2. Sauté onion and celery in oil/butter until soft. Add garlic, sage, and thyme; cook 2 more minutes.
3. In a large bowl, combine bread cubes, chestnuts, sautéed mix, and stock. Stir well to moisten.
4. Season, transfer to a greased baking dish, and bake uncovered 30–35 minutes until golden.

A hearty, grounding dish—this stuffing channels earth energy and abundance, perfect for Yule feasts.

Herbed Winter Solstice Pie

Ingredients
(Serves 6–8)

- 2 tbsp butter
- 1 leek, sliced
- 2 garlic cloves, minced
- 300g mixed winter greens (e.g. kale, spinach, chard), chopped
- 250g ricotta
- 100g feta, crumbled
- Zest of 1 lemon
- 2 eggs
- Salt and pepper
- 1 sheet shortcrust pastry

Method

1. Preheat oven to 180°C (350°F). Grease a pie dish.
2. Sauté leek and garlic in butter until soft. Add greens and wilt. Cool.
3. Mix greens with cheeses, lemon zest, eggs, salt, and pepper.
4. Line dish with pastry, add filling, and bake for 35–40 minutes until golden.

This vibrant pie represents renewal, with leafy greens calling in health and growth for the year ahead. Serve warm with gratitude.

Honey-Glazed Roast Root Vegetables

Ingredients
(Serves 4–6 as a side)

- 2 carrots, sliced
- 2 parsnips, sliced
- 1 sweet potato, cubed
- 1 red onion, cut into wedges
- 2 tbsp olive oil
- 1 tbsp honey
- 1 tsp fresh rosemary or thyme
- Salt and pepper

Method

1. Preheat oven to 200°C (400°F).
2. Place all vegetables on a tray. Drizzle with oil and honey. Sprinkle with herbs, salt, and pepper.
3. Toss to coat.
4. Roast for 30–40 minutes, turning once, until golden and tender.

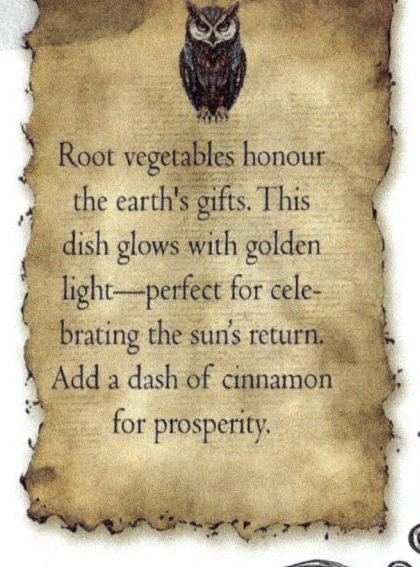

Root vegetables honour the earth's gifts. This dish glows with golden light—perfect for celebrating the sun's return. Add a dash of cinnamon for prosperity.

Slow Cooker Solstice Roast

Ingredients
(Serves 6–8)

- 1.5–2 kg (3–4 lb) beef chuck or lamb shoulder roast
- 4 garlic cloves, sliced
- 1 onion, sliced
- 3 carrots, cut in chunks
- 3 parsnips, cut in chunks
- 1 tbsp tomato paste
- 500ml (2 cups) beef stock
- 125ml (½ cup) red wine (optional)
- 2 tsp rosemary
- 1 tsp thyme
- Salt and pepper

Method

1. Brown roast on all sides in hot skillet (optional but flavorful).
2. Add all ingredients to slow cooker. Cook on low 8–10 hours or high 4–6 hours.
3. Remove meat, shred or slice. Serve with veg and pan juices.

Let this meal slow-cook while you enjoy your Yule rituals. It fills the house with warmth and cheer.

Winter Root Vegetable and Barley Bake

Ingredients
(Serves 6)

- 1 cup pearl barley
- 2 tbsp olive oil
- 1 onion, chopped
- 2 carrots, diced
- 1 parsnip, diced
- 1 turnip, diced
- 2 garlic cloves, minced
- 2 cups vegetable broth
- 1 tsp dried sage
- Salt and pepper
- ½ cup grated cheese (optional)

Method

1. Preheat oven to 180°C (350°F).
2. Cook barley in water until tender (30–40 minutes). Drain.
3. Sauté onion and garlic in oil. Add root veg and cook 10 minutes.
4. Stir in barley, broth, sage, salt, and pepper. Transfer to baking dish.
5. Top with cheese if using. Bake for 25–30 minutes.

Barley is sacred to winter and harvest gods, and this warming dish offers comfort and resilience—nourishing body and spirit through the cold.

Gingerbread Trifle

Ingredients
(Serves 8–10)

For gingerbread:
- 200g (1¾ cups) plain flour
- 1 tsp ground ginger
- ½ tsp cinnamon
- ½ tsp baking soda
- ½ tsp salt
- 115g (½ cup) butter
- 100g (½ cup) brown sugar
- 1 egg
- 160ml (2/3 cup) molasses
- 120ml (½ cup) hot water

For layers:
- 500ml (2 cups) whipping cream
- 2 tbsp icing sugar
- 1 tsp vanilla
- 300g (10 oz) stewed apples or spiced fruit compote
- Crushed ginger biscuits or nuts for topping

This trifle is rich with spice and memory. Serve in clear glass to show off the layers—like strata of the year gone by.

Method

1. Bake gingerbread: Mix dry ingredients. Cream butter and sugar. Add egg and molasses. Stir in dry ingredients and hot water. Bake in greased dish at 180°C (350°F) for 30–35 mins. Cool.
2. Whip cream with sugar and vanilla until soft peaks form.
3. In a trifle bowl, layer chunks of gingerbread, fruit, and cream. Repeat layers.
4. Top with crushed biscuits or chopped pecans. Chill before serving.

Honey & Cardamom Baked Pears

Ingredients
(Serves 4)

- 4 ripe pears, halved and cored
- 4 tbsp honey
- ½ tsp ground cardamom
- 2 tbsp chopped walnuts or pecans
- Optional: dollop of cream or yoghurt to serve

Elegant and easy—let these gently spiced pears enchant your Yule table.

Method

1. Preheat oven to 180°C (350°F). Place pears cut side up in a baking dish.
2. Drizzle with honey, sprinkle cardamom and nuts.
3. Bake 25–30 minutes until soft and golden.
4. Serve warm with cream or yoghurt.

Peppermint Bark Brownie Bites

Ingredients
(Makes 16 squares)

- ½ cup butter
- 200g dark chocolate, chopped
- ¾ cup sugar
- 2 eggs
- 1 tsp vanilla extract
- ½ cup plain flour
- Pinch of salt
- Topping:
  o 100g white chocolate, melted
  o Crushed peppermint candy or candy canes

Method

1. Preheat oven to 180°C (350°F). Line an 8x8" pan.
2. Melt butter and dark chocolate together. Let cool slightly.
3. Stir in sugar, eggs, and vanilla.
4. Mix in flour and salt.
5. Pour into tin and bake 20–25 minutes. Cool completely.
6. Spread with melted white chocolate and sprinkle with peppermint. Let set before slicing.

These minty bites are festive, energising, and a little bit magical. Peppermint clears the mind and chocolate lifts the heart—just what Yule calls for

Peppermint Bark

Ingredients
(Makes one tray, breaks into 20–25 pieces)

- 200g dark chocolate
- 200g white chocolate
- ½ tsp peppermint extract
- 4 crushed peppermint candy canes or mints

Method

1. Line a tray with baking paper.
2. Melt dark chocolate, stir in half the peppermint extract, and spread thinly over tray. Chill to set.
3. Melt white chocolate, stir in remaining extract, and pour over dark layer.
4. Sprinkle crushed candy on top.
5. Chill until firm, then break into shards.

Simple and striking, this treat is perfect for gifting or placing in a festive jar by the fire.

Snowflake Sugar Cookies

Ingredients
(Makes 24 cookies)

- 225g (1 cup) unsalted butter, softened
- 200g (1 cup) caster sugar
- 1 egg
- 1 tsp vanilla extract
- ½ tsp almond extract (optional)
- 300g (2½ cups) plain flour
- ½ tsp baking powder
- ¼ tsp salt

Method

1. Cream butter and sugar. Add egg, vanilla, and almond.
2. Stir in flour, baking powder, and salt. Mix to form dough.
3. Chill 1 hour. Preheat oven to 180°C (350°F).
4. Roll to ¼ inch thick. Cut into snowflake or star shapes.
5. Bake 8–10 mins until edges just begin to color. Cool on rack.
6. Decorate with icing or sugar sprinkles if desired.

Snowflakes represent the beauty in uniqueness—no two cookies or witches alike!

Spiced Apple Crumble Bars

Ingredients
(Makes 12 bars)

- 2 cups rolled oats
- 1 cup plain flour
- ½ cup brown sugar
- ½ tsp cinnamon
- ½ cup cold butter, cubed
- 2 cups stewed spiced apples (or thick apple sauce)

Method

1. Preheat oven to 180°C (350°F). Line a square baking tin.
2. Combine oats, flour, sugar, and cinnamon. Rub in butter until crumbly.
3. Press half the mixture into the tin. Spread apples over.
4. Sprinkle remaining crumble on top.
5. Bake for 35–40 minutes. Cool before slicing.

Perfect for feasting or packing for a winter solstice walk—spiced, rustic, and satisfying.

Spiced Solstice Shortbread

Ingredients
(Makes 24 small cookies)

- 1 cup (225g) unsalted butter, softened
- ½ cup icing sugar
- 1½ cups plain flour
- ½ cup rice flour or cornflour
- ½ tsp cinnamon
- ¼ tsp ground cardamom
- Pinch of salt

Method

1. Preheat oven to 160°C (320°F). Line a tray with baking paper.
2. Cream butter and sugar until light.
3. Sift in flours, spices, and salt. Mix until a dough forms.
4. Roll out and cut into shapes or press into a pan and score.
5. Bake for 20–25 minutes or until pale gold. Cool on a wire rack.

Simple yet sacred, these shortbread biscuits are perfect for ritual offerings or quiet tea-time spells. Cardamom brings warmth and clarity—ideal for reflection

Yule Spice Cookies

Ingredients
(Makes approx. 2 dozen)

- 2½ cups plain flour
- 1 tsp baking soda
- 1 tsp cinnamon
- ½ tsp ground ginger
- ½ tsp ground cloves
- ½ tsp nutmeg
- ½ tsp salt
- ¾ cup butter, softened
- 1 cup brown sugar
- ¼ cup molasses
- 1 egg
- 1 tsp vanilla extract

Method

1. Preheat oven to 180°C (350°F). Line baking trays with parchment paper.
2. In a bowl, mix flour, baking soda, spices, and salt.
3. In another bowl, beat butter and sugar until fluffy. Add molasses, egg, and vanilla.
4. Gradually mix in dry ingredients to form a soft dough.
5. Roll into small balls and flatten slightly.
6. Bake 8–10 minutes or until edges are golden. Cool on tray.

Infused with traditional Yule spices, these cookies fill your home with warmth and are perfect for sharing during solstice celebrations or leaving as offerings.

Chocolate Peppermint Elixir

Ingredients
(Serves 2)

- 2 cups milk (or plant-based)
- 100g dark chocolate, chopped
- 1 tsp peppermint extract
- Pinch of salt
- Whipped cream (optional)

Method

1. Heat milk in a pot. Add chocolate and stir until melted.
2. Stir in peppermint and salt.
3. Pour into mugs, top with whipped cream if desired.

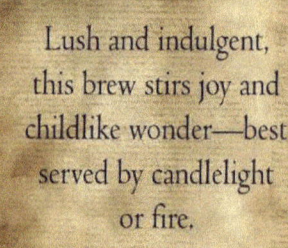

Lush and indulgent, this brew stirs joy and childlike wonder—best served by candlelight or fire.

Mulled Mead

Ingredients
(Serves 4)

- 1 bottle of mead (750ml)
- 1 small orange, sliced
- 2 cinnamon sticks
- 2 star anise
- 4 cloves
- Honey to taste (optional)

Honoring old traditions, this warm mead is a powerful solar drink—great for toasting the rebirth of light.

Method

1. Combine all ingredients in a saucepan.
2. Gently heat over low (do not boil) for 20 minutes.
3. Strain and serve warm in mugs.

Spiced Cranberry Punch

Ingredients
(Serves 6–8)

- 4 cups cranberry juice
- 2 cups apple juice
- 1 orange, sliced
- 4 whole cloves
- 2 cinnamon sticks
- ½ tsp ground ginger
- Optional: 1 cup sparkling water or dry cider for fizz

A tart-sweet celebration of the returning sun—perfect for ritual toasts or sharing with kindred spirits.

Method

1. Combine juices, orange slices, and spices in a pot.
2. Simmer gently for 15–20 minutes.
3. Remove from heat and strain if desired.
4. Add fizz just before serving. Serve warm or chilled.

Winter Solstice Wassail

Ingredients
(Serves 6–8)

- 1L apple cider
- 500ml orange juice
- 1 apple, sliced
- 1 orange, sliced
- 2 cinnamon sticks
- 5 cloves
- 1 tsp allspice
- Optional: dash of rum or brandy

A classic of Yuletide cheer—raise your cup and sing, for the light is returning!

Method

1. Combine all ingredients in a large pot.
2. Simmer gently for 30 minutes.
3. Ladle into mugs, adding spirits if desired.

Yule Herbal Chai

Ingredients
(Serves 2–3)

- 2 cups water
- 1 cinnamon stick
- 4 whole cardamom pods
- 4 whole cloves
- ½ tsp fennel seeds
- ½ tsp dried ginger
- 1 tbsp loose black tea (or 2 bags)
- 1½ cups milk (or oat milk)
- Honey to taste

Method

1. Simmer spices in water for 10 minutes.
2. Add tea and simmer 3 more minutes.
3. Add milk and warm through.
4. Strain and sweeten with honey.

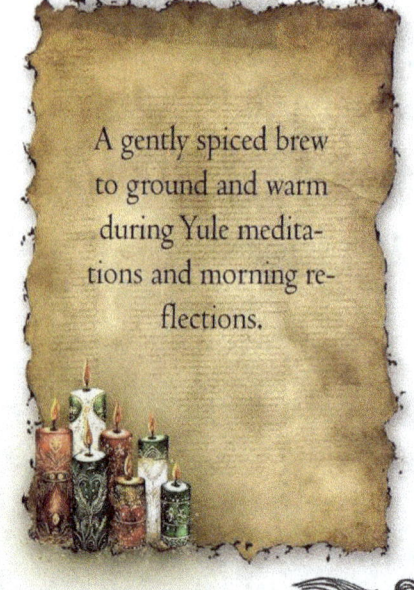

A gently spiced brew to ground and warm during Yule meditations and morning reflections.

Caramelized Onion & Cranberry Relish

Ingredients
(Fills 1 jar)

- 2 large onions, thinly sliced
- 1 tbsp olive oil or butter
- ½ cup dried cranberries
- 1 tbsp brown sugar
- 1 tbsp balsamic vinegar
- Pinch of salt

Method

1. Sauté onions in oil over low heat until deeply golden (20–25 minutes).
2. Stir in cranberries, sugar, vinegar, and salt. Simmer for 5 minutes.
3. Cool and store in a jar. Keeps in fridge for up to 1 week.

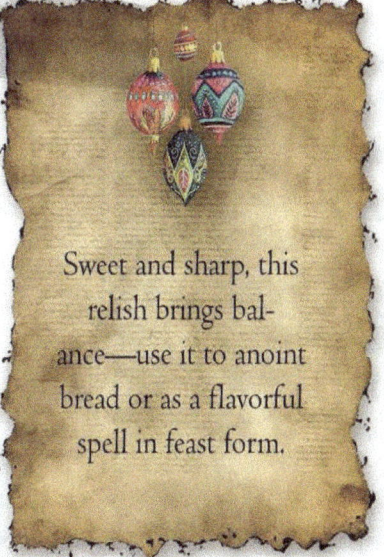

Sweet and sharp, this relish brings balance—use it to anoint bread or as a flavorful spell in feast form.

Solstice Herbed Salt Blend

Ingredients
(Fills 1 small jar)

- ½ cup coarse sea salt
- 2 tsp dried rosemary
- 2 tsp dried thyme
- 1 tsp dried orange zest (or lemon zest)
- Optional: ½ tsp dried sage or garlic granules

Method

1. Mix all ingredients in a bowl.
2. Store in a clean jar. Let sit a few days before using to infuse.
3. Use on roasted veg, breads, or grilled meats.

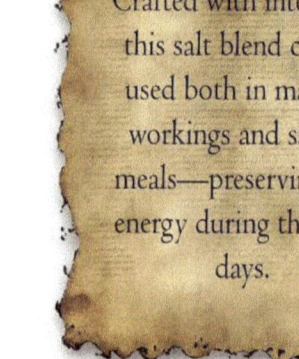

Crafted with intention, this salt blend can be used both in magical workings and sacred meals—preserving sun energy during the dark days.

Ingredients

Method

Imbolc: A Feast of Light and Renewal

Imbolc, celebrated on or around February 1st in the Northern Hemisphere, August 1st or 2nd in the Southern Hemisphere, marks the midpoint between the Winter Solstice and the Spring Equinox. It is a sacred turning point in the Wheel of the Year — a quiet but powerful celebration of returning light, new life stirring beneath the frozen earth, and the promise of spring to come.

Traditionally associated with Brigid, the Celtic goddess of hearth, healing, and fertility, Imbolc was a time to honor the sacred feminine, tend the home fires, and prepare for the agricultural season ahead. Brigid's connection to dairy animals, especially ewes, makes milk, butter, and cheese traditional offerings, while grains, seeds, and stored roots reflect the practical fare of winter pantries.

Food at Imbolc is both symbolic and sustaining — a ritual of hope and nourishment. These recipes are crafted with that spirit in mind: warming soups and hearty breads to chase away the cold, citrus and honey to awaken the senses, and sweets to celebrate the returning sun. Whether you are cooking for a quiet evening, a ritual feast, or a gathering with kindred souls, may this collection bring comfort, inspiration, and a touch of seasonal magic to your table.

Let the hearth be your altar.
Let the act of cooking be your offering.
And may the turning of the wheel bless your home with light.

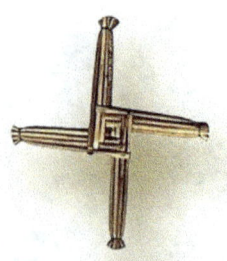

Imbolc Invocation

Brigid, keeper of the sacred flame,
Lady of the forge, the well, the womb,
We welcome your light in the hush of winter.
We call to you as the earth begins to stir.

Bless this hearth, this home, this table.
Bless the hands that gather, mix, and knead.
Let every spoonful carry warmth,
And every crumb be touched with hope.

As the milk flows and the seeds are sown,
May our spirits be nourished and renewed.
As fire crackles and candles burn,
May creativity awaken and intentions rise.

By bread and honey, root and spice,
We honor the season's gentle promise.
Light returns, and with it, life.
So may it be.

Imbolc Blessing

May the first light of Imbolc
Kindle hope within your heart.
May the hearth be warm,
The table full,
And your spirit nourished by simple joys.

May Brigid's flame bless your hands,
Your craft,
Your dreams not yet born.
May seeds you plant—within and without—
Find fertile ground and gentle rain.

As winter softens and the wheel turns,
May you walk in light,
Speak with love,
And rise each day with purpose.

Blessed Imbolc, and bright beginnings to you.

Brigid's Braided Bread

Ingredients
(Makes 1 braided loaf)

- 3 cups plain flour
- 1 tsp salt
- 2 tsp sugar
- 1 packet (7g) instant yeast
- 1 cup warm milk
- 2 tbsp olive oil
- 1 egg (for glaze)

Method

- Mix flour, salt, sugar, and yeast in a bowl. Add warm milk and oil.
- Knead into a soft dough. Cover and let rise until doubled (about 1 hour).
- Divide into 3 parts and roll into ropes. Braid and tuck ends under.
- Place on baking tray, cover, and rise again for 30 minutes.
- Brush with beaten egg and bake at 180°C (350°F) for 25–30 mins.

Braiding bread honors Brigid, goddess of hearth and home. Bake in her name to invite creativity and healing into your space.

Honeyed Oat Cakes

Ingredients
(Makes 12 small cakes)

- 1 ½ cups rolled oats
- ½ cup plain flour
- ½ tsp baking soda
- ¼ tsp salt
- ½ cup butter (softened)
- 1/3 cup honey
- 1 tbsp brown sugar

Oats for nourishment, honey for blessing — these simple treats honour Brigid's hearth and offer a golden sweetness to your Imbolc altar.

Method

- Preheat oven to 180°C (350°F).
- Mix oats, flour, baking soda, and salt.
- Cream butter, honey, and sugar, then stir into dry ingredients.
- Shape into small rounds and flatten slightly.
- Bake on a lined tray for 10–12 minutes or until golden. Cool on rack.

Milk and Herb Bread Rolls

Ingredients
(Makes 8 rolls)

- 3 cups strong bread flour
- 1 tsp salt
- 1 tbsp sugar
- 1 tbsp fresh rosemary or thyme, chopped
- 1 packet (7g) instant yeast
- 1 cup warm milk
- 2 tbsp melted butter

Method

- Mix dry ingredients and herbs in a bowl. Add warm milk and butter.
- Knead until smooth and elastic. Cover and rise for 1 hour.
- Divide into 8 balls. Place on a tray and rise again 30 mins.
- Bake at 180°C (350°F) for 20–25 minutes until golden.

Milk and herbs were sacred at Imbolc. These soft rolls bring together the nourishing and the sacred, ideal for ritual feasting.

Cinnamon Apple Braided Bread

Ingredients
(Makes 1 loaf)

- 2 ½ cups plain flour
- 2 tbsp sugar
- 1 tsp cinnamon
- 1 tsp dry yeast
- ¾ cup warm milk
- 2 tbsp butter, melted
- 1 apple, finely chopped
- 1 tbsp brown sugar

Method

- Combine yeast, warm milk, and sugar. Let sit 5–10 mins.
- Mix in flour, cinnamon, melted butter, and knead to form soft dough.
- Let rise 1 hour. Roll dough into rectangle, spread with chopped apple and brown sugar.
- Roll up, slice lengthwise, and twist into a braid.
- Let rise 30 mins, then bake at 180°C (350°F) for 25–30 minutes.

A beautiful loaf for sharing or offering. Braiding bread at Imbolc is a simple kitchen spell for unity, growth, and weaving blessings into the season ahead.

Herbed Cheese & Seed Crackers

Ingredients
(Makes approx. 24 small crackers)

- 1 cup plain flour
- 2 tbsp mixed seeds (sesame, flax, poppy)
- ¼ cup grated hard cheese (like parmesan or aged cheddar)
- 1 tsp dried herbs (thyme, rosemary)
- ¼ tsp salt
- 3 tbsp olive oil
- 3–4 tbsp cold water

Crisp, savoury, and symbolic of seeds stirring underground — these crackers are lovely for ritual feasts or Imbolc cheese boards.

Method

- Mix all dry ingredients. Stir in oil and water to form a dough.
- Roll thin and cut into shapes. Prick with fork.
- Bake at 180°C (350°F) for 12–15 minutes, until crisp and golden.

Oat and Honey Bannocks

Ingredients
(Makes 6 small rounds)

- 1 ½ cups rolled oats
- ¾ cup flour (plain or wholemeal)
- ½ tsp baking soda
- ¼ tsp salt
- ¼ cup unsalted butter, chilled
- 2 tbsp honey
- ½ cup buttermilk

Method

- Preheat oven to 190°C (375°F). Line a tray with baking paper.
- In a bowl, mix oats, flour, soda, and salt. Rub in the butter.
- Stir in honey and buttermilk to make a soft dough.
- Divide into 6 rounds and flatten slightly.
- Bake for 18–20 minutes until golden. Cool on a wire rack.

Oats and honey were traditional Imbolc offerings. These bannocks are perfect with butter or soft cheese and can be left at a threshold for Brigid's blessing.

Sun Wheel Scones

Ingredients
(Makes 8 wedges)

- 2 cups self-raising flour
- ¼ tsp salt
- 50g cold butter, cubed
- 1/3 cup sugar
- Zest of 1 lemon
- ½ cup milk
- 1 egg

Shaped like the sun, these zesty scones brighten the still-cold days. Serve with lemon curd or honey at your Imbolc table.

Method

- Preheat oven to 200°C (400°F). Grease a baking tray.
- Rub butter into flour and salt until crumbly. Stir in sugar and zest.
- Mix milk and egg; add most to form a dough. Keep a little to glaze.
- Pat into a circle, score into 8 wedges, and glaze.
- Bake for 15–18 minutes until golden.

Baked Cauliflower & White Bean Gratin

Ingredients
(Serves 4–6)

- 1 small head cauliflower, cut into florets
- 1 can white beans, drained
- 2 tbsp olive oil
- 1 tsp mustard
- ¾ cup grated cheese (cheddar or parmesan)
- ¼ cup breadcrumbs
- Salt, pepper, pinch of nutmeg

Method

- Preheat oven to 180°C (350°F).
- Steam cauliflower until just tender.
- In a bowl, mix beans, mustard, oil, salt, pepper, and a pinch of nutmeg.
- Add cauliflower and half the cheese. Mix gently.
- Pour into baking dish, top with breadcrumbs and remaining cheese.
- Bake for 20–25 minutes until bubbling and golden.

Cauliflower's pale blooms and nourishing beans make this a sacred kitchen dish—symbolic of purity and promise. Bake it with intention.

Brigid's Flame Pie
(Leek & Cheese Pie)

Ingredients
(Serves 6–8)

- 1 sheet shortcrust pastry
- 2 large leeks, sliced
- 1 tbsp butter
- 3 eggs
- 1 cup cream or milk
- 1 ½ cups grated cheese (cheddar or gruyère)
- Salt, pepper, pinch of thyme

Method

- Preheat oven to 180°C (350°F).
- Sauté leeks in butter until soft. Cool slightly.
- Beat eggs with cream, season, and stir in cheese and thyme.
- Line a pie dish with pastry, add leek mixture, then egg mixture.
- Bake for 30–35 minutes until set and golden.

Leeks and dairy are sacred to Brigid. This pie, golden like the flame, is perfect for family dinners or offerings by candlelight.

Candlemas Cheese & Herb Tartlets

Ingredients
(Makes 6 tartlets)

- 1 sheet puff pastry
- 1 cup ricotta or cream cheese
- 1 egg yolk
- 1 tsp dried mixed herbs (or chopped fresh)
- Salt and pepper
- Optional: sprinkle of crumbled feta or seeds

Method

- Preheat oven to 200°C (400°F).
- Cut pastry into 6 squares and place into a greased muffin tin or tartlet pans.
- Mix cheese, yolk, herbs, and seasonings.
- Fill each pastry case and top with feta or seeds if using.
- Bake for 15–18 minutes until puffed and golden.

These golden tartlets evoke little suns. Serve them warm beside candles for a celebratory Imbolc brunch or light supper.

Fire-Roasted Red Pepper & Goat Cheese Galette

Ingredients
(Serves 4–6)

- 1 sheet shortcrust or puff pastry
- 2 red bell peppers, roasted and sliced
- 1 small red onion, thinly sliced
- 100g goat cheese (or feta)
- 1 tbsp olive oil
- 1 tsp thyme
- 1 egg (for egg wash)
- Salt & pepper

Method

- Preheat oven to 200°C (400°F).
- On a baking tray, lay out pastry and arrange peppers, onion, and crumbled goat cheese in the center, leaving a 5cm border.
- Drizzle with olive oil, sprinkle thyme, salt, and pepper.
- Fold the edges inward to create a rustic galette. Brush edges with beaten egg.
- Bake for 25–30 minutes until golden and crisp.

With the colours of flame and sun, this open-faced galette is a visual spell for returning warmth. A perfect centerpiece for Imbolc feasts.

Imbolc Shepherd's Bake
(with Lentils & Roots)

Ingredients
(Serves 6)

- 1 tbsp olive oil
- 1 onion, chopped
- 2 garlic cloves, minced
- 2 cups cooked lentils (green or brown)
- 1 carrot and 1 parsnip, grated
- 1 tbsp tomato paste
- 1 tsp dried sage
- ½ cup vegetable stock
- 3–4 cups mashed potatoes (butter optional)

Method

- Preheat oven to 190°C (375°F).
- Sauté onion and garlic in oil. Add veg, lentils, tomato paste, sage, and stock.
- Simmer until thickened (about 10 minutes).
- Spread into a baking dish, top with mashed potatoes, and smooth or fork.
- Bake for 25–30 minutes until golden and bubbling.

Comforting and frugal, this dish echoes the season's themes of warmth, patience, and transformation. A good one to bless before sharing.

Brigid's Hearth Baked Rice Pudding

Ingredients
(Serves 4–6)

- 1 cup uncooked rice (short grain)
- 4 cups milk
- ½ cup sugar
- 1 tsp vanilla or orange blossom water
- ½ tsp cinnamon
- Butter for greasing
- Optional: raisins or orange zest

Method

- Preheat oven to 160°C (320°F).
- Grease a baking dish. Combine rice, milk, sugar, and vanilla.
- Pour into dish, sprinkle cinnamon, dot with butter.
- Bake uncovered for 1.5–2 hours, stirring halfway.
- Add raisins or zest for extra flavour if desired.

This creamy, comforting pudding echoes Brigid's gentle nurturing flame — a humble hearth dish to share with loved ones or honour the Goddess.

Honey & Oat Brittle

Ingredients
(Makes one sheet — breaks into 12–16 shards)

- ½ cup rolled oats
- ½ cup chopped nuts (hazelnuts or almonds work well)
- ¾ cup honey
- Pinch of salt
- ½ tsp cinnamon

Method

- Lightly toast oats and nuts in a dry pan until golden.
- In a saucepan, heat honey with salt and cinnamon until bubbling.
- Stir in oats and nuts. Pour onto a parchment-lined tray and spread thinly.
- Let cool completely, then break into rustic shards.

Golden and nourishing, this treat echoes the returning sun and Brigid's sacred grains. A perfect energy booster for early spring workings or gifting.

Imbolc Milk Pudding
with Spiced Pears

Ingredients
(Serves 4–6)

- 3 cups milk
- 1/3 cup sugar
- ½ cup fine semolina or ground rice
- 1 tsp vanilla extract
- 2 ripe pears, sliced
- 1 tbsp butter
- 1 tbsp brown sugar
- ½ tsp cinnamon

Method

- In a saucepan, heat milk and sugar to a simmer.
- Whisk in semolina, stirring constantly until thickened (5–7 mins).
- Stir in vanilla. Spoon into bowls.
- In another pan, cook pears in butter, brown sugar, and cinnamon until soft and golden.
- Top each pudding with warm pears.

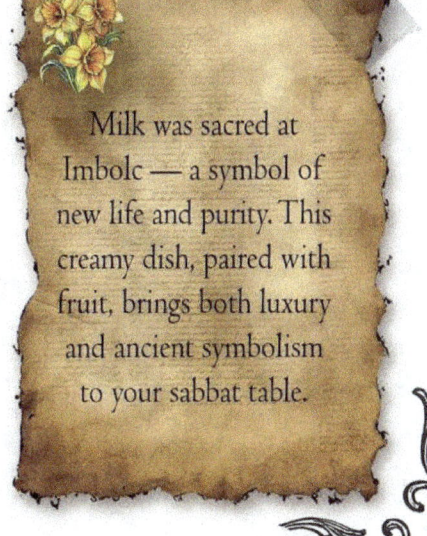

Milk was sacred at Imbolc — a symbol of new life and purity. This creamy dish, paired with fruit, brings both luxury and ancient symbolism to your sabbat table.

Spiced Custard Tarts

Ingredients
(Makes 6 small tarts)

- 1 sheet shortcrust pastry
- 2 egg yolks
- 2 tbsp sugar
- ½ tsp ground cinnamon
- ¼ tsp nutmeg
- 1 cup milk
- ½ tsp vanilla extract

Method

- Preheat oven to 180°C (350°F). Grease a muffin tray.
- Cut pastry to fit 6 muffin holes. Chill 10 mins.
- Warm milk with spices. Beat yolks, sugar, and vanilla, then whisk in warm milk slowly.
- Pour into pastry shells. Bake for 20–25 mins until just set. Cool completely.

Golden, rich, and spiced—these little tarts echo the returning sun and are a sweet offering to Brigid, guardian of inspiration and hearth.

White Chocolate & Lavender Bark

Ingredients
(Makes 1 tray, breaks into shards)

- 200g white chocolate
- 1 tsp dried culinary lavender
- Optional: edible glitter or rose petals

Method

- Melt chocolate gently in a double boiler or microwave.
- Pour onto a lined tray and spread thin.
- Sprinkle with lavender and optional extras.
- Chill until firm, then break into shards.

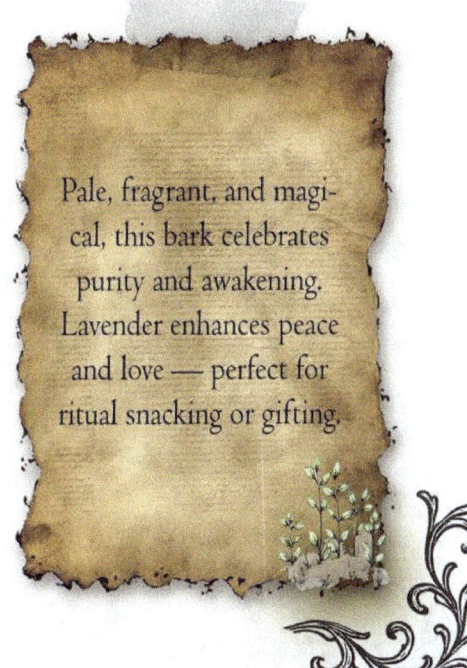

Pale, fragrant, and magical, this bark celebrates purity and awakening. Lavender enhances peace and love — perfect for ritual snacking or gifting.

Brigid's Blessing Milk Tea

Ingredients
(Serves 2)

- 2 cups milk (dairy or plant-based)
- 1 tsp dried chamomile
- 1 tsp dried lavender
- 1 tsp dried lemon balm
- 1 tsp honey (or more to taste)

Method

- Warm milk gently in a saucepan — do not boil.
- Stir in herbs and allow to steep for 5–7 minutes.
- Strain into mugs, sweeten with honey, and serve warm.

Milk honours Brigid's nourishing energy, while calming herbs ease the mind for visioning the season ahead. Perfect for post-ritual reflection or evening

Creamy Vanilla Oat Nog

Ingredients
(Serves 2–3)

- 2 cups oat milk
- 1 egg yolk (or 1 tbsp cornstarch for vegan)
- 2 tbsp maple syrup
- 1 tsp vanilla extract
- Pinch of nutmeg

Method

- Whisk all ingredients in a saucepan over medium heat until gently thickened.
- Serve warm or chilled, with a sprinkle of nutmeg.

This cozy, spiced drink calls in comfort and clarity. Vanilla invokes harmony, while oat and spice soothe and centre the spirit as the wheel turns.

Golden Oat Moon Milk

Ingredients
(Serves 2)

- 2 cups oat milk
- ½ tsp ground turmeric
- ¼ tsp cinnamon
- Pinch of ground ginger
- 1 tsp maple syrup or honey
- Optional: pinch of black pepper

Method

- Heat all ingredients in a pan over low heat, whisking until warm and blended.
- Pour into mugs and drink slowly.

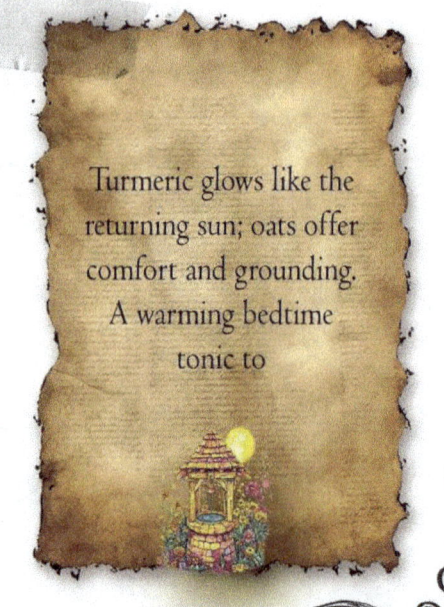

Turmeric glows like the returning sun; oats offer comfort and grounding. A warming bedtime tonic to

Imbolc Mulled White Wine

Ingredients
(Serves 4–6)

- 1 bottle white wine (dry or semi-sweet)
- 2 tbsp honey
- 2 cinnamon sticks
- 4 cardamom pods
- 1 star anise
- 1 tsp dried chamomile or elderflower
- ½ orange, sliced

A sun-bright twist on traditional mulled wine. Elderflower and chamomile add magic and clarity — a warming drink to welcome the sun's return.

Method

- Combine all ingredients in a saucepan and gently heat (do not boil).
- Simmer on low for 15–20 minutes.
- Strain and serve warm.

Fairy Lavender Wine

Ingredients
Makes approx. 1 bottle

- 750ml white wine (dry or semi-sweet)
- 2 tbsp dried culinary lavender (or ¼ cup fresh blossoms)
- Zest of 1 small lemon
- 2 tbsp honey (or to taste)
- Optional: edible flowers or fresh lavender sprigs for garnish

Method

1. Gently warm the wine in a saucepan over low heat—do not let it boil.
2. Add lavender and lemon zest. Remove from heat, cover, and let steep for 30–45 minutes.
3. Strain through a fine mesh or muslin into a clean jug.
4. Stir in honey while still slightly warm, adjusting sweetness to taste.
5. Pour into a clean bottle or jar and chill before serving.
6. Garnish with a few floating edible petals or a lavender sprig if desired.

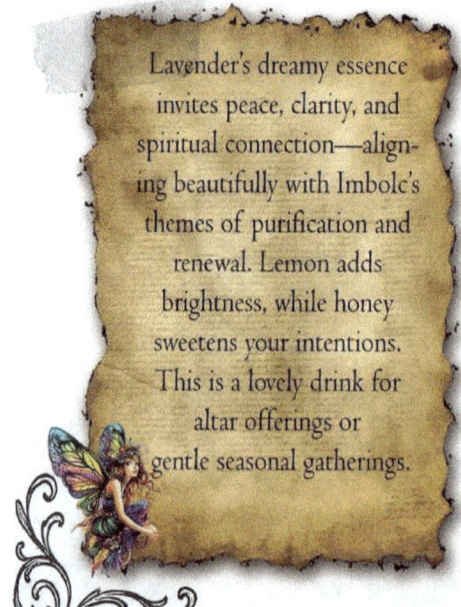

Lavender's dreamy essence invites peace, clarity, and spiritual connection—aligning beautifully with Imbolc's themes of purification and renewal. Lemon adds brightness, while honey sweetens your intentions. This is a lovely drink for altar offerings or gentle seasonal gatherings.

Lemon Balm & Honey Hearth Tonic

Ingredients
(Serves 2–3)

- 2 cups hot water
- 2 tsp dried lemon balm
- 1 tsp dried mint
- 1 tbsp honey
- 1 tsp lemon juice

Bright and herbaceous, this simple tonic clears the winter fog. Lemon balm is sacred to Brigid and invites peace, healing, and lightness.

Method

- Steep lemon balm and mint in hot water for 10 minutes.
- Strain, then stir in honey and lemon juice.
- Serve warm, or chilled with ice and lemon slices.

Citrus & Chamomile Marmalade

Ingredients
(Fills 3–4 small jars)

- 2 large oranges
- 1 lemon
- 1 cup water
- 1½ cups sugar
- 1 tbsp dried chamomile flowers

Method

- Thinly slice oranges and lemon, removing seeds.
- Simmer with water until peel is tender (about 30 mins).
- Stir in sugar and chamomile, then boil until set (15–20 mins).
- Spoon into sterilised jars and seal.

Citrus brightens the spirit and chamomile soothes — a perfect preserve for Imbolc's return of light and warmth. Wonderful on toast with a morning blessing.

Honey Butter Spread

Ingredients
(Fills 2 small jars)

- 1 cup unsalted butter, room temperature
- ¼ cup honey
- 1 tsp vanilla extract
- Pinch of cinnamon

Method

- Beat all ingredients until smooth and fluffy.
- Spoon into clean jars and refrigerate.

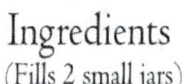

Silky and golden, this honey butter celebrates Brigid's connection to dairy and bees. Ideal for Imbolc feasting or gifting to friends with fresh bread.

Lemon & Thyme Jelly

Ingredients
(Fills 3 small jars)

- 1½ cups lemon juice
- 1 tbsp lemon zest
- 2½ cups sugar
- 3 tbsp fresh thyme leaves
- 1 pouch liquid pectin

Method

- Combine lemon juice, zest, sugar, and thyme. Bring to a boil.
- Stir in pectin and boil hard for 1–2 mins.
- Pour into sterilised jars and seal.

Bright and herbal, this jelly balances sharpness and sweetness — symbolic of the old and new seasons meeting. Excellent with cheese or in ritual offerings.

Milk & Rose Petal Jam
(Egyptian-Style)

Ingredients
(Fills 2–3 small jars)

- 2 cups whole milk
- 1 cup sugar
- 1 cup rose petals (edible, unsprayed)
- ½ tsp lemon juice

Method

- Simmer milk and sugar until reduced and thickened.
- Stir in petals and lemon juice; simmer until petals soften and mixture is jammy.
- Spoon into jars and refrigerate.

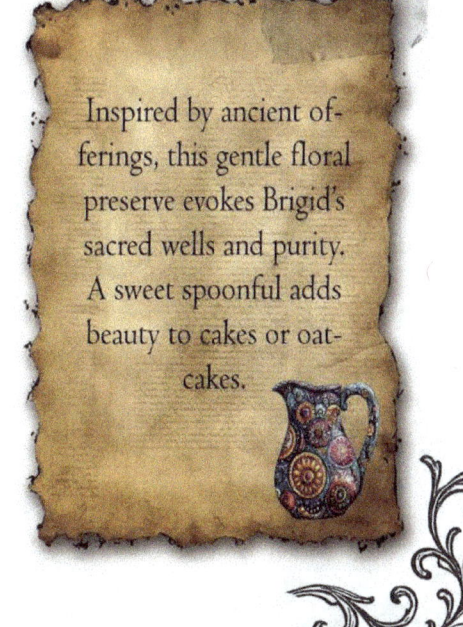

Inspired by ancient offerings, this gentle floral preserve evokes Brigid's sacred wells and purity. A sweet spoonful adds beauty to cakes or oatcakes.

Vanilla Pear Preserve

Ingredients
(Fills 3–4 small jars)

- 4 ripe pears, peeled, cored, and chopped
- 1½ cups sugar
- Juice of 1 lemon
- 1 vanilla bean (or 1 tsp vanilla extract)
- ½ cup water

Method

- Combine pears, sugar, lemon juice, and water in a saucepan.
- Split and scrape vanilla bean, adding both seeds and pod to the pan.
- Simmer gently until pears are soft and syrup thickens (30–40 mins).
- Remove vanilla pod. Spoon into sterilised jars and seal.

This soft, light-hued preserve brings together the sweetness of pear and the nurturing warmth of vanilla — an elegant treat for Brigid's feast and perfect for Imbolc blessings.

Ingredients

Method

Ostara : Welcoming the Light

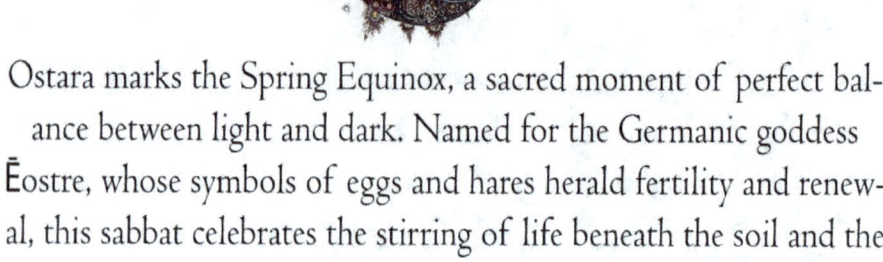

Ostara marks the Spring Equinox, a sacred moment of perfect balance between light and dark. Named for the Germanic goddess Ēostre, whose symbols of eggs and hares herald fertility and renewal, this sabbat celebrates the stirring of life beneath the soil and the first bold blooms of the season.

As the sun strengthens and days grow longer, the earth awakens in joyful colour. Buds swell, birds return, and the fresh scent of green things fills the air. It is a time of beginnings—of planting seeds both literal and spiritual, of setting intentions, and of celebrating the promise of growth.

In kitchens, Ostara is honoured with seasonal ingredients: tender greens, fresh herbs, eggs, honey, and floral notes. These foods echo the energy of the season—bright, cleansing, and full of potential. Whether you're baking for a feast, preparing offerings, or simply welcoming spring into your home, these recipes are crafted to nourish both body and spirit.

May these Ostara dishes bring joy to your table, warmth to your hearth, and blessings to all who share them with you.

Invocation to Ostara

Ostara, Lady of the dawn,
Bright goddess of Spring reborn,
We call to You as light and life return—
As blossoms burst and green fires burn.

Come with the breeze that stirs the trees,
With the song of birds and hum of bees.
Bless our hearths, our hands, our seed,
With joy, with hope, with all we need.

Goddess of hare, of egg, of flower,
Awaken the world with Your gentle power.
In this season of balance, growth, and cheer,
Ostara, we welcome You—be near.

Ostara Kitchen Blessing

As light returns and green things grow,
May these recipes bless all those who know
The joy of sharing food with grace,
And find the Spring in every place.

With eggs and herbs, with sun-warmed bread,
With sweets and feasts so lovingly spread,
Let every bite, both bold and small,
Bring peace and plenty to us all.

Blessed be this Ostara tide,
Where warmth and wisdom now abide.

Bird's Nest Macaroons

Ingredients
(Makes 12 nests)

- 2 ½ cups shredded coconut
- ¾ cup sweetened condensed milk
- 1 tsp vanilla extract
- 1 egg white
- Small candy-coated eggs (or berries)

Method

1. Mix coconut, condensed milk, and vanilla in a bowl.
2. Whip egg white to soft peaks, fold into coconut mixture.
3. Scoop heaped tablespoons onto a lined tray, shaping into nest forms.
4. Bake at 170°C (340°F) for 15–18 minutes, until golden. Cool completely.
5. Place candy eggs in the centre of each nest.

Perfect for children's altars or treats, these sweet nests symbolize fertility and rebirth at the turning of the wheel.

Carrot & Honey Mini Loaves

Ingredients
(Makes 6 mini loaves or 1 large loaf)
- 2 cups grated carrot
- 2 cups plain flour
- 1 tsp baking soda
- ½ tsp salt
- 1 tsp cinnamon
- ½ tsp ground ginger
- 2 eggs
- ½ cup honey
- ½ cup oil (sunflower or mild olive)
- 1 tsp vanilla extract
- ½ cup chopped walnuts or seeds (optional)

Method

1. Preheat oven to 175°C (350°F). Grease mini loaf pans or one large pan.
2. In one bowl, mix flour, baking soda, salt, and spices.
3. In another bowl, beat eggs, honey, oil, and vanilla. Stir in carrots.
4. Combine wet and dry mixtures. Fold in nuts or seeds if using.
5. Spoon into pans and bake 25–30 minutes for minis (50–55 minutes for a large loaf), until a skewer comes out clean.
6. Cool on a rack before slicing.

Carrots, sweetened with golden honey, bring earth and sun together — a perfect offering to honour the balance of Ostara.

Ostara Blossom Muffins

Ingredients
(Makes 12 muffins)

- 2 cups self-raising flour
- ½ tsp cinnamon
- ½ cup sugar
- 1 egg
- ¾ cup milk
- 1/3 cup oil
- ½ tsp vanilla extract
- ½ cup apple (grated)
- ¼ cup edible flowers (e.g., violets, primrose, calendula)

Method

1. Preheat oven to 180°C (350°F). Line a muffin tin.
2. In a bowl, mix flour, cinnamon, and sugar.
3. In another bowl, beat egg with milk, oil, and vanilla.
4. Combine wet and dry ingredients, fold in grated apple and edible petals.
5. Spoon into cases and bake for 18–20 minutes or until risen and golden.

Celebrate the bloom of spring with floral muffins that honour nature's first offerings. Choose safe, edible blossoms to match the energy of the season.

Ostara Egg Bread Nests

Ingredients
(Makes 6 individual nests)

- 2 ½ cups plain flour
- 2 ¼ tsp (1 packet) instant yeast
- ¼ cup sugar
- ½ tsp salt
- ¾ cup warm milk
- 2 tbsp butter, melted
- 1 egg
- 6 dyed or natural eggs (uncooked)
- Optional: sesame or poppy seeds for topping

Method

1. In a large bowl, combine flour, yeast, sugar, and salt.
2. Stir in warm milk, butter, and egg until a dough forms. Knead for 8–10 minutes until smooth.
3. Cover and let rise in a warm place for 1 hour or until doubled.
4. Divide dough into 6 pieces. Roll each into a rope and twist into a circle to form a nest.
5. Place each nest on a lined baking tray. Gently nestle one egg in the centre of each (they will cook as the bread bakes).
6. Cover and let rise another 20 minutes. Preheat oven to 180°C (350°F).
7. Brush with milk and sprinkle with seeds if using. Bake for 20–25 minutes until golden.

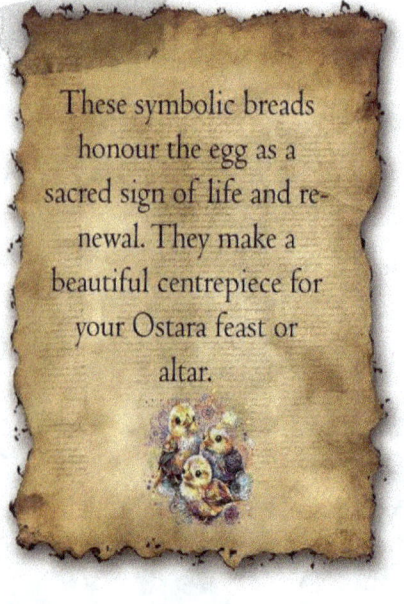

These symbolic breads honour the egg as a sacred sign of life and renewal. They make a beautiful centrepiece for your Ostara feast or altar.

Ostara Seed Cake

Ingredients
(Makes one small loaf or 8 slices)
- 1 cup plain flour
- ½ cup sugar
- ½ cup butter, softened
- 2 eggs
- 1 tbsp milk
- 1 tsp baking powder
- 1 tbsp caraway seeds
- Zest of ½ lemon (optional)

Method

1. Preheat oven to 175°C (350°F). Grease and line a small loaf tin.
2. Cream butter and sugar together until light and fluffy.
3. Beat in the eggs one at a time, adding a spoonful of flour if it begins to curdle.
4. Stir in milk, then fold in flour, baking powder, seeds, and lemon zest if using.
5. Pour into the tin and smooth the top.
6. Bake for 40–45 minutes or until a skewer comes out clean. Cool in tin 10 mins, then turn out.

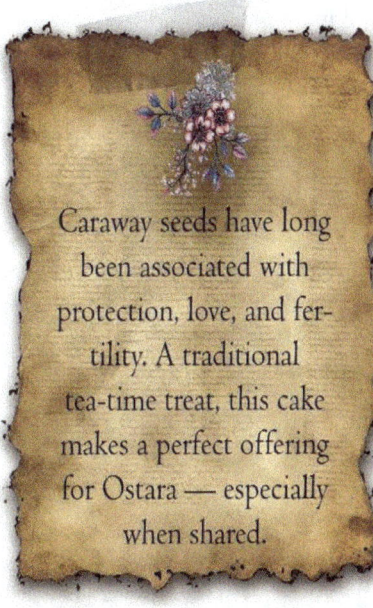

Caraway seeds have long been associated with protection, love, and fertility. A traditional tea-time treat, this cake makes a perfect offering for Ostara — especially when shared.

Spring Herb Scones

Ingredients
((Makes 8 wedges))

- 2 cups self-raising flour
- ½ tsp salt
- 1 tsp mustard powder
- 100g cold butter, cubed
- ¾ cup milk
- 1 tbsp chopped fresh chives
- 1 tbsp chopped fresh parsley
- Optional: crumbled feta or grated cheese

Method

1. Preheat oven to 200°C (390°F). Line a tray with baking paper.
2. In a large bowl, mix flour, salt, and mustard powder. Rub in butter until crumbly.
3. Stir in herbs (and cheese, if using). Add milk gradually, mixing to a soft dough.
4. Turn onto a floured surface, gently shape into a circle about 2cm thick.
5. Cut into 8 wedges and place on tray slightly apart.
6. Brush with a little extra milk and bake 12–15 minutes until golden.

These scones celebrate the fresh greens of spring. Ideal for your Ostara picnic or alongside soups at the sabbat table.

Spring Onion & Feta Flatbreads

Ingredients
(Makes 4)

- 1½ cups plain flour
- ½ cup Greek yogurt
- ½ tsp baking powder
- Pinch of salt
- 2 spring onions, finely chopped
- ½ cup crumbled feta cheese
- Olive oil for cooking

Warm, soft, and full of spring flavour, these are ideal for scooping dips or serving alongside Ostara stews and soups.

Method

1. Mix flour, baking powder, salt, yogurt, and spring onions into a dough.
2. Divide into 4 pieces, roll out flat. Press crumbled feta into the dough.
3. Heat a skillet with a little oil. Cook flatbreads 2–3 mins per side until golden.

Bacon & Spring Onion Quiche

Ingredients
(Serves 6–8)

- 1 shortcrust pastry shell
- 4 eggs
- 1 cup cream or milk
- 1 cup grated cheese (cheddar or Swiss)
- 6 rashers streaky bacon, chopped
- ½ cup chopped spring onions
- Salt, pepper, pinch of nutmeg

Method

1. Preheat oven to 180°C (350°F). Blind bake pastry for 10 mins.
2. Fry bacon until crisp. Whisk eggs, cream, and seasonings together.
3. Add bacon, onions, and cheese to crust. Pour egg mix over.
4. Bake for 25–30 mins until golden and set.

Eggs are central to Ostara lore—this quiche is both hearty and symbolic, perfect for brunch or feasting.

Chickpea & Lemon Skillet Stew

Ingredients
(Serves 4)

- 1 tbsp olive oil
- 1 onion, diced
- 2 garlic cloves, minced
- 1 can chickpeas, drained
- 2 cups vegetable broth
- Zest & juice of 1 lemon
- 1 cup chopped kale or spring greens
- Salt, pepper, pinch of turmeric
- Optional: yogurt or tahini drizzle to serve

Method

1. Sauté onion and garlic in oil until soft.
2. Add chickpeas, broth, lemon zest, juice, and turmeric. Simmer 10 mins.
3. Stir in greens, cook 2–3 mins until wilted.
4. Season and serve with drizzle of choice

Bright with lemon and golden warmth, this stew encourages clarity and renewal—excellent for cleansing after winter's rest.

Devilled Eggs
with Spring Herbs & Flowers

Ingredients
(Makes 6 servings)

- 6 large eggs
- 2 tbsp mayonnaise
- 1 tsp Dijon mustard
- 1 tsp apple cider vinegar
- Salt & pepper to taste
- 1 tbsp finely chopped dill or chives
- Edible flowers (e.g., viola, nasturtium) for garnish

Method

1. Hard-boil eggs (10 minutes), cool, and peel. Halve and scoop yolks into a bowl.
2. Mash yolks with mayo, mustard, vinegar, salt, and pepper until smooth.
3. Pipe or spoon into whites. Top with herbs and a tiny edible flower.

Elegant and playful, these devilled eggs are perfect for Ostara gatherings, symbolising the sacred balance of light and dark..

Herbed Spring Lamb Chops

Ingredients
(Serves 4)

- 8 lamb cutlets or chops
- 2 tbsp olive oil
- 2 garlic cloves, minced
- 1 tbsp fresh rosemary, chopped
- 1 tbsp fresh thyme, chopped
- Zest of 1 lemon
- Salt & pepper
- Optional: edible flowers for garnish

Method

1. Mix oil, garlic, herbs, lemon zest, salt and pepper into a marinade.
2. Rub lamb chops with mixture and marinate for 30 minutes or longer.
3. Grill or pan-sear chops for 3–4 minutes per side, or until done to your liking.
4. Rest briefly, then serve with spring vegetables or herbed couscous.

Lamb, a sacred animal of the season, honours the awakening earth and traditional Ostara feasting.

Honey-Mustard Glazed Chicken
with Spring Vegetables

Ingredients
(Serves 4–6)

- 1 whole chicken (or 4–6 thighs/drumsticks)
- 2 tbsp wholegrain mustard
- 2 tbsp honey
- 1 tbsp apple cider vinegar
- 2 tbsp olive oil
- 4 baby carrots, sliced lengthways
- 8 small new potatoes
- 1 cup sugar snap peas or green beans
- Salt & pepper

Method

1. Preheat oven to 200°C (400°F).
2. Mix mustard, honey, vinegar, and oil.
3. Place chicken in a baking dish, brush with glaze. Add carrots and potatoes.
4. Roast for 40–50 minutes, adding peas or beans in the last 10 minutes.
5. Spoon glaze over everything before serving.

A bright, balanced meal with sweet and sharp notes—perfect for Ostara, when daylight and darkness are equal.

Ostara Herb & Ricotta Tart

Ingredients
(Serves 6–8)

- 1 sheet shortcrust pastry
- 1½ cups ricotta cheese
- 2 eggs
- 1 cup chopped mixed herbs (sorrel, parsley, chives, tarragon)
- Salt, pepper, and a pinch of nutmeg
- Optional: edible flower petals to garnish

Method

1. Preheat oven to 180°C (350°F). Line a tart pan with pastry. Prick and blind bake for 10 minutes.
2. Mix ricotta, eggs, herbs, salt, pepper, and nutmeg.
3. Pour filling into crust. Bake for 25–30 mins or until just set.
4. Cool slightly before slicing. Garnish with petals if desired.

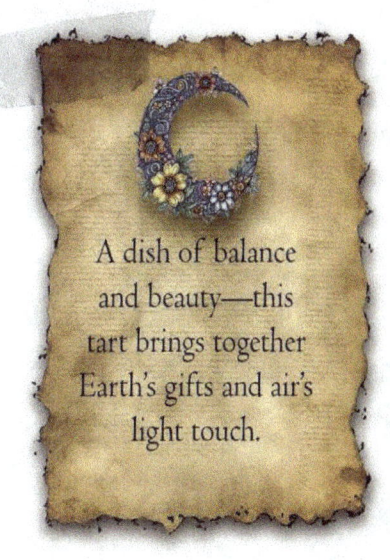

A dish of balance and beauty—this tart brings together Earth's gifts and air's light touch.

Pickled Quail Eggs
with Spring Herbs

Ingredients
(Makes 12–16 eggs)

- 12–16 quail eggs
- 1 cup white wine vinegar
- ½ cup water
- 1 tsp salt
- 1 tsp sugar
- 1 tsp pink peppercorns
- 1 tsp mustard seeds
- 2 sprigs fresh dill
- 1 small sprig rosemary
- 1 tsp chopped chives

Eggs are ancient Ostara symbols of fertility and potential. These tiny orbs are delicious on spring platters or served as part of a ritual meal.

Method

1. Boil quail eggs for 4 minutes, then plunge into cold water and peel.
2. Combine vinegar, water, salt, sugar, and spices in a saucepan. Simmer for 2–3 minutes, then let cool slightly.
3. Place eggs in a sterilised jar with herbs and chives. Pour brine over to cover.
4. Seal and refrigerate for at least 2 days before eating.

Rabbit & Root Vegetable Pie

Ingredients
(Serves 4–6)

- 500g rabbit meat (or chicken if preferred), diced
- 1 onion, chopped
- 2 carrots, chopped
- 1 parsnip or small turnip, diced
- 2 cloves garlic
- 1 tbsp flour
- 1 cup vegetable or chicken stock
- 1 tbsp cream (optional)
- 1 tbsp chopped fresh thyme
- Salt & pepper
- 1 sheet puff pastry

Method

1. Preheat oven to 180°C (350°F).
2. Sauté rabbit and vegetables until browned. Add garlic and thyme.
3. Stir in flour, then stock and cream. Simmer until thickened.
4. Pour into baking dish and top with puff pastry. Bake 25–30 minutes.

A nod to traditional countryside fare, this hearty pie celebrates abundance, rebirth, and the hunt's end.

Smoked Fish & Herb Cakes

Ingredients
(Makes 6–8 cakes)

- 250g cooked smoked fish (e.g. cod, trout, or salmon), flaked
- 1 cup mashed potatoes
- 1 egg
- ¼ cup breadcrumbs
- 2 tbsp chopped fresh herbs (parsley, dill)
- Zest of 1 lemon
- Salt & pepper
- Oil or butter for frying

> Fish connects to flowing water, intuition, and new life—especially fitting for early spring and balance rituals.

Method

1. Mix all ingredients until well combined. Form into small cakes.
2. Chill for 20 minutes if possible to firm up.
3. Fry in oil or butter until golden on both sides.

Spring Green Frittata

Ingredients
(Serves 4)

- 6 eggs
- ½ cup milk or cream
- 1 cup chopped baby spinach
- ½ cup chopped asparagus
- ¼ cup chopped fresh herbs (chives, parsley, dill)
- ½ cup crumbled feta or goat cheese
- Salt & pepper to taste
- 1 tbsp olive oil

Method

1. Preheat oven to 180°C (350°F).
2. Whisk eggs and milk with salt, pepper, and herbs.
3. Heat oil in an oven-safe skillet. Sauté spinach and asparagus for 2–3 mins.
4. Pour egg mixture over veggies, sprinkle with cheese.
5. Cook on stove until edges set, then transfer to oven for 10–15 mins until golden.

Eggs symbolise fertility and rebirth—this vibrant dish makes a lovely offering for dawn rituals or brunch feasts.

Spring Pea & Mint Dip

Ingredients
(Makes about 1 cup)

- 200g frozen or fresh peas, cooked
- 1 small garlic clove
- 2 tbsp Greek yogurt or plant-based yogurt
- 1 tbsp lemon juice
- 1 tbsp olive oil
- 4–5 fresh mint leaves
- Salt and pepper to taste

Method

1. Blend all ingredients until smooth and creamy.
2. Adjust seasoning and lemon to taste.
3. Chill before serving with crackers or veggie sticks.

Fresh, green, and zingy—this dip is bursting with life. Perfect for Ostara feasts, picnics, or balancing a rich main.

Stuffed Portobello Mushrooms
with Barley & Herb Medley

Ingredients
(Serves 2–4)

- 4 large Portobello mushrooms
- 1 cup cooked barley
- 2 tbsp olive oil
- 2 garlic cloves, minced
- ½ cup chopped spring herbs (parsley, mint, chervil)
- ½ cup finely chopped nuts (walnuts or hazelnuts)
- Zest of 1 lemon
- Salt & pepper

Method

1. Preheat oven to 190°C (375°F).
2. Remove mushroom stems. Brush caps with oil and place on baking tray.
3. Sauté garlic in oil, then stir into barley with herbs, nuts, zest, salt and pepper.
4. Spoon filling into mushrooms and bake 20–25 mins.

Earthy and nourishing, these stuffed mushrooms celebrate the awakening land and the return of fresh green life.

Wild Garlic & Potato Cakes

Ingredients
(Makes 6–8 small cakes)

- 2 cups mashed potatoes (cooled)
- ½ cup chopped wild garlic or spring onions
- ½ cup grated cheese (cheddar or parmesan)
- 1 egg
- ½ cup flour or bread-crumbs
- Salt & pepper
- Oil for frying

Method

1. Mix mashed potato, garlic, cheese, and egg. Season.
2. Shape into small patties and coat lightly in flour or crumbs.
3. Fry in oil over medium heat until golden on both sides.

> Wild garlic is one of the earliest greens to appear, symbolising protection and vitality—perfect for Ostara celebrations.

Honey & Chamomile Custards

Ingredients
(Makes 4 small ramekins)

- 1 ½ cups whole milk
- 3 chamomile tea bags (or 3 tsp dried chamomile flowers)
- 3 egg yolks
- ¼ cup honey
- ½ tsp vanilla extract
- Pinch of salt

Method

1. Gently heat milk in a saucepan until just below boiling. Remove from heat and steep chamomile for 10 minutes. Strain.
2. Whisk egg yolks, honey, vanilla, and salt in a bowl.
3. Slowly pour warm milk into egg mixture while whisking.
4. Pour into ramekins. Place in a baking dish and add hot water halfway up the sides.
5. Bake at 150°C (300°F) for 30–35 mins, until set with a slight wobble. Chill before serving.

These floral, golden custards honour the honeybees and calming herbs of spring. Lovely for Ostara brunch or after ritual feasting.

Honey-Ricotta Stuffed Dates
with Pistachio Crumble

Ingredients
(Makes 12)
- 12 Medjool dates, pitted
- ½ cup ricotta cheese
- 1 tbsp honey
- ¼ tsp cinnamon
- 2 tbsp crushed pistachios

Method

1. Mix ricotta, honey, and cinnamon until smooth.
2. Carefully open each date and spoon in filling.
3. Top with a sprinkle of crushed pistachios. Chill before serving.

Sweet and rich, these little bites call in sweetness for the season ahead. Ideal for spring feasts or as a charming kitchen witch treat.

Lemon Curd Tartlets

Ingredients
(Makes 12 tartlets)

- 12 mini pastry shells (store-bought or homemade)
- 3 large eggs
- ½ cup lemon juice
- Zest of 1 lemon
- ½ cup sugar
- ¼ cup butter

Bright and zesty, lemon curd is perfect for Ostara—a sun-drenched treat celebrating the returning light.

Method

1. Whisk eggs, juice, zest, and sugar in a saucepan.
2. Cook over low heat, stirring constantly, until thick.
3. Stir in butter until smooth.
4. Spoon into tart shells. Chill before serving.

Ostara Carrot Truffles

Ingredients
(Makes about 20 truffles)

- 1 cup finely grated carrot
- ½ cup crushed digestive biscuits or graham crackers
- ½ cup ground almonds
- ¼ cup cream cheese
- 2 tbsp maple syrup or honey
- ½ tsp cinnamon
- White chocolate or coconut (for coating)

Earthy and sweet, these truffles embody the planting energy of Ostara, blending rabbit lore with natural goodness.

Method

1. Mix all ingredients in a bowl until a thick dough forms.
2. Roll into balls. Chill for 30 minutes.
3. Dip in melted white chocolate or roll in desiccated coconut.
4. Refrigerate until set.

Ostara Fruit Leathers

Ingredients
(Makes about 12 strips)

- 500g fresh or frozen strawberries or raspberries
- 2 tbsp honey or maple syrup
- 1 tsp lemon juice

Naturally sweet and great for little ones' Ostara picnics. Use seasonal fruits as they become available.

Method

1. Blend all ingredients until smooth.
2. Pour onto a silicone mat or baking paper, spread thinly.
3. Dry in a dehydrator or oven at lowest heat (around 60°C / 140°F) for 4–6 hours until just tacky.
4. Cut into strips and roll up in parchment.

Sheep-Shaped Honey Cookies

Ingredients
(Makes approx. 20)

- ½ cup softened butter
- ¼ cup honey
- ¼ cup brown sugar
- 1 egg
- 1 ¾ cups plain flour
- ½ tsp cinnamon
- ¼ tsp baking soda
- Icing sugar (optional, for decoration)

Method

1. Cream butter, honey, and sugar. Add egg and mix well.
2. Stir in flour, cinnamon, and baking soda. Chill for 1 hour.
3. Roll out and cut into sheep shapes.
4. Bake at 180°C (350°F) for 8–10 mins. Cool and dust or ice if desired.

These cookies honour spring lambs, sacred to many Ostara traditions. Offer one on your altar or share with kin.

Sugared Candied Nuts

Ingredients
(Makes about 2 cups)

- 200g mixed nuts (almonds, walnuts, pecans)
- 1 egg white
- 100g caster sugar
- 1/2 tsp cinnamon
- Pinch of salt

Method

1. Whisk the egg white until frothy. Stir in nuts to coat.
2. Mix sugar, cinnamon, and salt, then toss with the nuts.
3. Spread on a lined tray and bake at 150°C (300°F) for 30–35 mins, stirring once.
4. Let cool and store in an airtight jar.

Perfect for Ostara baskets or nibbling during springtime rituals. Enchant with intention while stirring.

Ostara Blossom Tea Blend

Ingredients
(Makes enough for 6–8 cups)

- 2 tbsp dried chamomile flowers
- 1 tbsp dried elderflower
- 1 tbsp dried lemon balm
- 1 tbsp dried rose petals
- 1 tsp dried lavender (optional)

Brew Ostara's bloom into your cup. This gentle, heart-opening tea is ideal for ritual, journaling, or sipping as you sow seeds.

Method

1. Mix herbs gently in a bowl and store in a sealed jar away from light.
2. To use, steep 1 heaped teaspoon per cup in hot water for 5–7 minutes.
3. Sweeten with honey or enjoy over ice.

Blossom Sugar Cubes

Ingredients
(Makes 12–20 cubes)

- 100g granulated sugar
- 1 tsp water
- Edible flowers (tiny blossoms like violets, forget-me-nots, primrose)

Method

1. Mix sugar and water until it resembles damp sand.
2. Press into silicone moulds, add a flower on top of each.
3. Let dry at room temp for 12–24 hours or oven dry on low.
4. Pop out and store in an airtight jar.

Use to sweeten Ostara teas and infuse your brews with floral energy and beauty.

Wild Garlic & Lemon Butter

Ingredients
(Makes about 1/2 cup)

- 100g unsalted butter, softened
- 1 small handful wild garlic leaves, finely chopped
- Zest of 1 lemon
- Pinch of salt

This verdant butter sings of spring! Use it to finish Ostara veggies, spread on warm bread, or stir into grain bowls.

Method

1. Mash the softened butter with the garlic, lemon zest, and salt until fully combined.
2. Spoon onto parchment paper and roll into a log. Chill until firm.
3. Slice as needed or store in the fridge for up to a week.

Ingredients

Method

Taste of Beltane
A Celebration of Fire, Fertility, and Abundance

Beltane — the festival of blossoming — arrives in a rush of colour, scent, and warmth. The air is rich with the perfume of hawthorn and the hum of bees, as Earth herself stirs in passionate embrace with the Sun. This is the time of sacred union, of maypoles and bonfires, of dancing feet and blooming hearts. A turning point in the Wheel of the Year, Beltane is the threshold of summer — a celebration of life's fertile abundance and the magic that ripens in the warming soil.

In ancient times, fires were lit on hilltops and cattle were driven between them for blessing and protection. Today, we honour Beltane with food that is sensual, joyful, and fresh — dishes kissed by herbs, blossoms, honey, and flame. These recipes are designed to capture that spirit: of passion and play, of vitality and renewal.

Within these pages, you'll find offerings for your Beltane table — vibrant salads adorned with edible flowers, fire-kissed breads and butters, meads and herbal cordials, and sweet confections worthy of faerie feasts. Whether you are gathering for a communal celebration, picnicking in a field of daisies, or simply creating sacred space in your kitchen, may these recipes nourish both body and soul.

Beltane Kitchen Invocation

In this sacred turning of the Wheel,
I stand at the threshold of fire and flower.
With open hands and steady heart,
I enter the kitchen — temple of creation.

Each ingredient I touch holds a whisper,
Each stir, a blessing.
I call in passion, joy, and new beginnings
As I chop, mix, knead, and flame.

Let love rise like steam from the pot,
Let healing steep in every brew.
Let laughter sweeten every bite,
And courage be baked into golden crust.

These dishes are more than sustenance —
They are spells cast with salt and flame,
Intention folded into every layer,
A feast that feeds both body and spirit.

As the fires of Beltane burn bright,
So too does the magic I stir into this meal.
May all who share in this feast
Be nourished, uplifted, and blessed.

So it is spoken. So it shall be.

Beltane Blessings

Let the wild things grow.
Let your laughter rise like smoke from a sacred fire.
Let your table bloom with colour, scent, and love.

This is a time to court pleasure — to gather herbs at dawn, to sip sparkling mead in the golden hour, to bake with your hands and dance barefoot on the grass.

Each dish in this collection is a little offering: to the Earth, to the fire, to the flowering of

Eat with intention. Share with joy.
And remember —
The magic begins the moment you light the stove.

Asparagus Puff Pastry Twists

Ingredients

- 1 sheet puff pastry (thawed if frozen)
- 12 thin asparagus spears, woody ends trimmed
- 1 egg, beaten (for egg wash)
- 1/4 cup grated parmesan or hard cheese of choice
- 1 tsp garlic powder
- 1 tsp dried thyme or rosemary
- Salt & pepper, to taste
- Optional: sesame seeds or poppy seeds for topping

Method

1. Preheat your oven to 200°C (400°F) and line a baking tray with parchment.
2. Roll out your puff pastry slightly and cut it into 12 strips.
3. Mix together parmesan, garlic powder, herbs, salt, and pepper in a bowl.
4. Sprinkle the cheese mixture evenly over the strips and lightly press it in.
5. Wrap each strip of pastry around an asparagus spear in a spiral twist.
6. Brush with egg wash, and sprinkle seeds on top if using.
7. Bake for 15–20 minutes or until golden brown and puffed.
8. Serve warm or cooled — perfect for dipping or as part of a festive platter!

Asparagus is a potent symbol of new life and vitality, making it a perfect Beltane offering. These twists are simple but look magical when served upright in a jar or bundled with herbs. Delightfully earthy and elegant!

Traditional Bannock

Ingredients

- 2 cups (250 g) all-purpose flour (or a mix of oat and barley flour for an old-world touch)
- 1 tsp baking soda
- ½ tsp salt
- 2 tbsp (28 g) butter or solid coconut oil (for a vegan option)
- ¾ cup (180 ml) buttermilk (or plant milk + 1 tsp vinegar for vegan)
- 1 tbsp honey or maple syrup (optional, for a slightly sweet version)
- A little extra flour for dusting and shaping
- Butter or oil for the skillet

Method

1. In a large bowl, mix together the flour, baking soda, and salt.
2. Cut in the butter or coconut oil until the mixture resembles coarse breadcrumbs.
3. Stir in the buttermilk (and honey, if using) until a soft dough forms. Don't overmix.
4. Turn the dough onto a floured surface and shape it into a round about ½ inch (1.25 cm) thick.
5. Score a cross into the top to divide into quarters—this was traditionally done to "let the fae out" and for even cooking.
6. Heat a heavy skillet or griddle over medium-low heat and grease lightly.
7. Cook the bannock for about 7–8 minutes per side, until golden and cooked through.
8. Slice into wedges and serve warm with butter, jam, or drizzled honey.

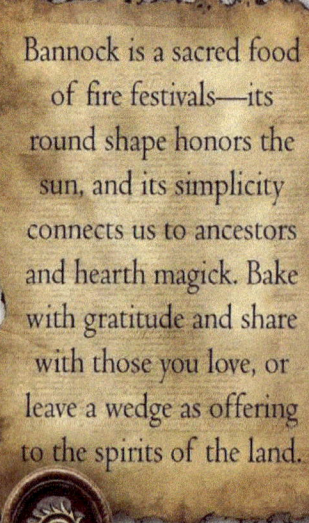

Bannock is a sacred food of fire festivals—its round shape honors the sun, and its simplicity connects us to ancestors and hearth magick. Bake with gratitude and share with those you love, or leave a wedge as offering to the spirits of the land.

Lemon Balm Scones with Honey Butter

Ingredients

- 2 cups (240 g) all-purpose flour
- ¼ cup (50 g) granulated sugar
- 1 tbsp baking powder
- ½ tsp salt
- Zest of 1 lemon
- ½ cup (113 g) cold unsalted butter, cubed
- ½ cup (120 ml) heavy cream (plus extra for brushing)
- 1 large egg
- 2 tbsp fresh lemon balm leaves, finely chopped
- 1 tsp vanilla extract

For the Honey Butter:

- ¼ cup (57 g) unsalted butter, softened
- 2 tbsp honey
- Pinch of salt

Method

1. Preheat oven to 400°F (200°C). Line a baking tray with parchment.
2. In a large bowl, whisk together flour, sugar, baking powder, salt, and lemon zest.
3. Cut in the cold butter using your fingertips or a pastry cutter until the mixture resembles coarse crumbs.
4. In a small bowl, whisk together cream, egg, lemon balm, and vanilla. Pour into the flour mixture.
5. Stir just until a shaggy dough forms—don't overmix.
6. Turn out onto a floured surface and gently pat into a 1-inch thick round.
7. Cut into 8 wedges (or use a cutter for rounds), and place on baking tray.
8. Brush tops with cream and bake for 15–18 minutes, until golden. Cool slightly.

Lemon balm is a herb of joy and calm—perfect for lifting the spirit. It brings lightness, clarity, and love. Use it in these Beltane scones to sweeten your celebrations and soothe any lingering winter heaviness.

To Make the Honey Butter:
Beat together butter, honey, and a pinch of salt until creamy and smooth.
Serve the warm scones with a generous spread of honey butter. Pure bliss.

Wild Garlic and Herb Bread

Ingredients

- 3 cups (360 g) all-purpose flour
- 2 tsp instant yeast
- 1 tsp salt
- 1 cup (240 ml) warm water
- 2 tbsp olive oil, plus extra for brushing
- 1 cup wild garlic leaves, finely chopped
- 2 tbsp fresh parsley, chopped
- 1 tbsp fresh thyme leaves (or 1 tsp dried)
- Optional: ½ cup grated hard cheese (like mature cheddar or parmesan)

Method

1. In a large mixing bowl, whisk together the flour, yeast, and salt.
2. Add the warm water and olive oil. Mix with a wooden spoon or hands until a shaggy dough forms.
3. Knead the dough on a floured surface for 8–10 minutes, until it becomes smooth and elastic.
4. Flatten the dough slightly, sprinkle in the wild garlic and herbs (and cheese if using), then fold and knead gently until evenly distributed.
5. Form into a ball and place in a lightly oiled bowl. Cover with a damp cloth and let rise in a warm spot for 1 hour, or until doubled in size.
6. Punch down the dough and shape into a round or oval loaf. Place on a parchment-lined baking tray.
7. Cover loosely and let rise for 30 minutes. Meanwhile, preheat oven to 375°F (190°C).
8. Slash the top with a sharp knife, brush with olive oil, and bake for 30–35 minutes, or until golden and the loaf sounds hollow when tapped. Cool on a wire rack. Serve warm with butter or

Wild garlic is abundant near Beltane, growing in shady woods and hedgerows. It brings purification, protection, and renewal—perfect for this season of blossoming energy. As you knead the dough, infuse it with wishes for abundance and vitality.

Floral Goat Cheese Dip
with Edible Blossoms and Honey Drizzle

Ingredients

- 200g (7 oz) soft goat cheese
- 2 tbsp cream cheese (for extra creaminess)
- 1 tbsp fresh lemon juice
- 1 tsp lemon zest
- 1 tbsp finely chopped chives
- Salt and freshly ground black pepper, to taste
- 2 tsp edible flower petals (like violets, nasturtiums, calendula, or rose)
- 2 tsp runny honey, for drizzling
- Optional: microgreens or extra herbs for garnish
- Crackers, crostini, or fresh bread, to serve

Method

1. In a bowl, blend the goat cheese, cream cheese, lemon juice, and zest until smooth and spreadable.
2. Stir in the chopped chives and season with salt and pepper to taste.
3. Gently fold in half of the edible flower petals, saving the rest for garnish.
4. Spoon the dip into a small serving bowl. Drizzle the top with honey and scatter remaining flower petals over it.
5. Garnish with a few extra herbs or microgreens for a fresh, wild look.
6. Serve with warm bread, crackers, or fresh veggies.

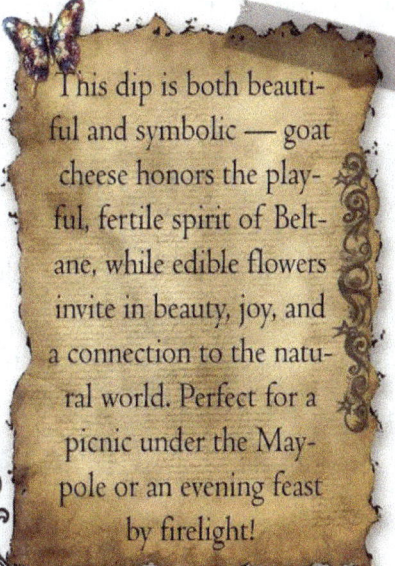

This dip is both beautiful and symbolic — goat cheese honors the playful, fertile spirit of Beltane, while edible flowers invite in beauty, joy, and a connection to the natural world. Perfect for a picnic under the Maypole or an evening feast by firelight!

Grilled Halloumi & Vegetable Skewers

Ingredients

- 1 block (225g / 8 oz) halloumi, cut into cubes
- 1 red bell pepper, chopped into chunks
- 1 zucchini, sliced into thick half-moons
- 1 small red onion, cut into wedges
- 6–8 cherry tomatoes
- 2 tbsp olive oil
- 1 tbsp lemon juice
- 1 garlic clove, minced
- 1 tsp dried oregano or thyme
- Salt & pepper, to taste
- Optional: a pinch of chili flakes or smoked paprika
- Bamboo or metal skewers (soak bamboo skewers for 20 mins before grilling)

Method

1. In a bowl, mix olive oil, lemon juice, garlic, herbs, salt, pepper, and optional chili flakes.
2. Toss the halloumi and veggies gently in the marinade. Let sit for 15–30 minutes for max flavor.
3. Thread halloumi and vegetables onto skewers, alternating colors and textures.
4. Preheat a grill, griddle pan, or barbecue. Grill skewers for about 8–10 minutes, turning occasionally, until veggies are tender and charred, and halloumi is golden.
5. Serve hot, garnished with fresh herbs or a drizzle of herbed yogurt or tahini.

Perfect for outdoor feasting! Halloumi, sacred to Mediterranean lands, holds the sun's warmth. These skewers are pure Beltane magic — fire-kissed and full of life. Serve under the open sky, where laughter and love gather like sparks.

Honey Glazed Roast Veggie Tart

Ingredients

- For the Tart Base:
- 1 sheet puff pastry (store-bought or homemade; vegan if needed)
- 1 tbsp olive oil
- 1 tsp Dijon mustard (optional, adds zing)

For the Filling:
- 1 small zucchini, sliced
- 1 red capsicum (bell pepper), sliced
- 1 red onion, sliced into petals
- 1 small sweet potato, thinly sliced or cubed
- 1 cup cherry tomatoes, halved
- 2 tbsp olive oil
- Salt & pepper, to taste
- 1 tsp dried thyme or rosemary

Honey Glaze:
- 1½ tbsp honey (use maple syrup or agave for vegan)
- 1 tsp balsamic vinegar
- ½ tsp smoked paprika

To Serve:
- A few edible flower petals (calendula, marigold, viola, etc.)
- Fresh basil or thyme leaves

Method

1. Preheat oven to 400°F (200°C). Line a tray with parchment paper.
2. Toss chopped vegetables in olive oil, salt, pepper, and dried herbs. Spread on a tray and roast for 20–25 minutes, until tender and slightly golden.
3. While roasting, whisk together the honey, balsamic vinegar, and smoked paprika to make your glaze.
4. Roll out the puff pastry onto a lined baking tray. Lightly score a border around the edge (about 1 inch from the sides) and prick the center with a fork.
5. Brush the inside of the tart base lightly with olive oil or Dijon mustard.
6. Arrange the roasted veggies on the tart base (inside the border), then drizzle with the glaze.
7. Bake the tart for 20–25 minutes until the edges puff and turn golden brown.
8. Cool slightly. Top with edible flowers and fresh herbs before serving warm or at room temperature.

Root veggies ground us, zucchini and tomatoes represent fertility and abundance, and honey (or its plant-based twin) brings warmth, healing, and golden joy. This tart is a celebration of the Earth's gifts—make it with intention, and eat it under sun or stars to welcome Beltane's fire.

Lamb & Rosemary Pies

Ingredients

- 300g (10 oz) minced lamb
- 1 small onion, finely chopped
- 1 garlic clove, minced
- 1 tbsp olive oil or butter
- 1 tbsp fresh rosemary, finely chopped (or 1 tsp dried)
- 1 tsp fresh thyme (optional)
- 1 tbsp tomato paste
- 2 tbsp stock or water
- Salt & pepper, to taste

For the Pastry:

- 1 sheet shortcrust or puff pastry (store-bought or homemade)
- 1 egg, beaten (for brushing) – or plant milk for vegan option
- Optional: sesame seeds or poppy seeds for sprinkling

Method

1. Preheat oven to 200°C (400°F).
2. Heat oil in a frying pan over medium heat. Add onion and cook until soft, then stir in garlic and lamb. Cook until browned.
3. Add rosemary, thyme, tomato paste, stock, salt and pepper. Simmer for 5–7 minutes, until mixture thickens slightly. Let cool.
4. Roll out pastry and cut into circles or ovals (about 10–12 cm / 4–5 inches across). Spoon filling onto one half of each piece.
5. Fold over, press edges with a fork to seal, and place on a baking tray lined with parchment.
6. Brush tops with beaten egg or plant milk, and sprinkle with seeds if using.
7. Bake for 20–25 minutes, until golden and crisp.

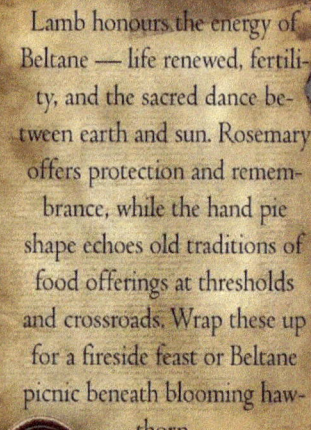

Lamb honours the energy of Beltane — life renewed, fertility, and the sacred dance between earth and sun. Rosemary offers protection and remembrance, while the hand pie shape echoes old traditions of food offerings at thresholds and crossroads. Wrap these up for a fireside feast or Beltane picnic beneath blooming hawthorn.

New Potato & Chive Salad
with creamy mustard dressing & dill

Ingredients

- 500g (about 1 lb) new potatoes, scrubbed and halved
- Salt, for boiling
- 3 tbsp fresh chives, finely chopped
- 2 tbsp fresh dill, chopped (or 1 tbsp dried)

For the Creamy Mustard Dressing:
- 3 tbsp sour cream or plain yogurt (plant-based works too)
- 1 tbsp wholegrain mustard
- 1 tsp apple cider vinegar or lemon juice
- 1 tsp olive oil
- Salt & pepper, to taste

Method

1. Boil the potatoes in salted water for 12–15 minutes, or until fork-tender. Drain and allow to cool slightly.
2. In a small bowl, mix together the dressing ingredients until smooth and creamy. Adjust seasoning to taste.
3. Place the warm (not hot) potatoes in a mixing bowl. Add the chives and dill, and gently fold in the dressing until everything is well coated.
4. Let sit for at least 10 minutes before serving to allow flavours to mingle. Delicious warm or chilled.

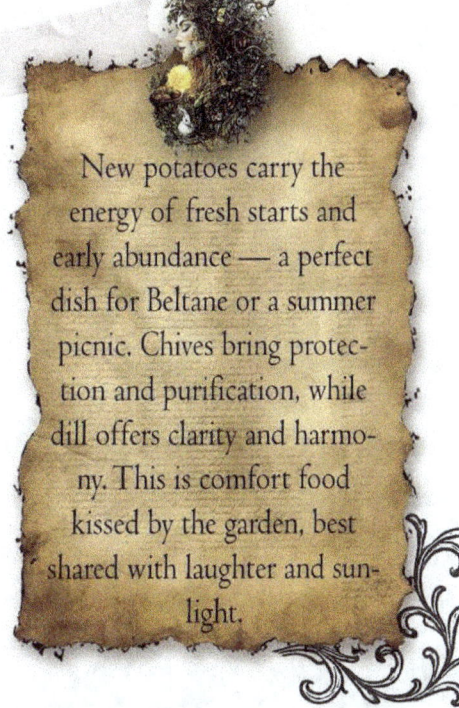

New potatoes carry the energy of fresh starts and early abundance — a perfect dish for Beltane or a summer picnic. Chives bring protection and purification, while dill offers clarity and harmony. This is comfort food kissed by the garden, best shared with laughter and sunlight.

Roasted Beet & Orange Salad

Ingredients

- 3 medium beets (red, golden, or a mix), peeled and chopped into wedges
- 1 tbsp olive oil
- Salt & pepper, to taste
- 2 oranges, peeled and sliced into rounds or segments
- 1/4 small red onion, thinly sliced
- 2 cups baby spinach or arugula
- 1/4 cup crumbled goat cheese or plant-based feta (optional)
- 2 tbsp toasted walnuts or pecans

For the Dressing:
- 2 tbsp olive oil
- 1 tbsp orange juice (fresh squeezed)
- 1 tsp apple cider vinegar or balsamic vinegar
- 1/2 tsp maple syrup or honey
- Pinch of salt

Method

1. Preheat oven to 200°C (400°F). Toss beet wedges with olive oil, salt, and pepper. Spread on a baking tray and roast for 30–35 minutes, until tender and caramelised at the edges. Let cool slightly.
2. In a small bowl, whisk together the dressing ingredients until smooth.
3. Arrange greens on a platter or shallow bowl. Layer with roasted beets, orange slices, and red onion.
4. Drizzle with dressing and gently toss to coat.
5. Top with goat cheese (if using), toasted nuts, and a crack of black pepper. Serve warm or at room temperature.

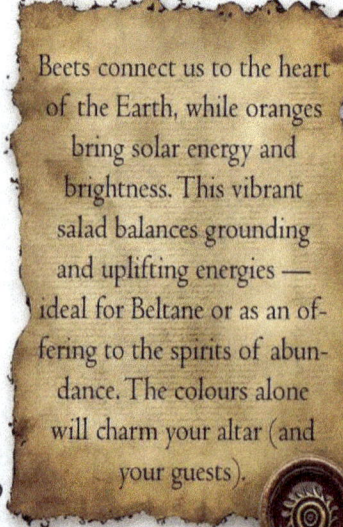

Beets connect us to the heart of the Earth, while oranges bring solar energy and brightness. This vibrant salad balances grounding and uplifting energies — ideal for Beltane or as an offering to the spirits of abundance. The colours alone will charm your altar (and your guests).

Rosemary-Honey Chicken
with Edible Flowers

Ingredients

- 6 bone-in, skin-on chicken thighs (or boneless thighs or breasts, if preferred)
- 3 tbsp olive oil
- 2 tbsp honey
- 1 tbsp lemon juice
- 2–3 garlic cloves, minced
- 1 tbsp fresh rosemary, finely chopped (or 1 tsp dried)
- ½ tsp smoked paprika
- ½ tsp salt
- ¼ tsp black pepper
- Optional: pinch of chili flakes for heat
- Edible flower petals for garnish (like nasturtium, calendula, marigold, violets, or rose)

Method

1. In a bowl, whisk together olive oil, honey, lemon juice, garlic, rosemary, paprika, salt, pepper, and chili flakes (if using).
2. Place chicken in a dish or ziplock bag. Pour marinade over, turning to coat well. Cover and marinate for at least 2 hours—or overnight in the fridge for deeper flavor.
3. Preheat oven to 400°F (200°C) or heat an outdoor grill to medium-high.
4. Roast chicken in a baking dish for 35–40 minutes, or grill for about 6–8 minutes per side, until cooked through and beautifully golden.
5. Rest for 5 minutes before serving. Sprinkle with edible flower petals and a little flaky salt just before bringing to the table.

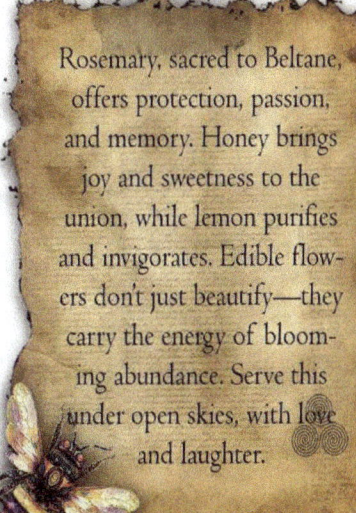

Rosemary, sacred to Beltane, offers protection, passion, and memory. Honey brings joy and sweetness to the union, while lemon purifies and invigorates. Edible flowers don't just beautify—they carry the energy of blooming abundance. Serve this under open skies, with love and laughter.

Spiced Root Veg Fritters

Ingredients

- 1 medium sweet potato, grated
- 1 medium carrot, grated
- 1 small parsnip or beetroot, grated
- 1 small onion, finely chopped
- 2 garlic cloves, minced
- 2 eggs
- 1/4 cup plain flour (or chickpea flour for gluten-free)
- 1/2 tsp ground cumin
- 1/2 tsp ground coriander
- 1/4 tsp smoked paprika
- Salt & pepper, to taste
- Olive oil or ghee, for frying

Method

1. Grate all root veggies into a bowl. Use a clean towel to squeeze out excess moisture.
2. Add onion, garlic, eggs, flour, spices, salt and pepper. Mix until well combined.
3. Heat a splash of oil in a frying pan over medium heat.
4. Drop spoonfuls of the mixture into the pan, flattening slightly with the back of the spoon.
5. Cook each fritter for 3–4 minutes on each side or until golden and cooked through.
6. Drain on paper towel and serve hot or cold — excellent with herbed yogurt, chutney, or honeyed mustard dip.

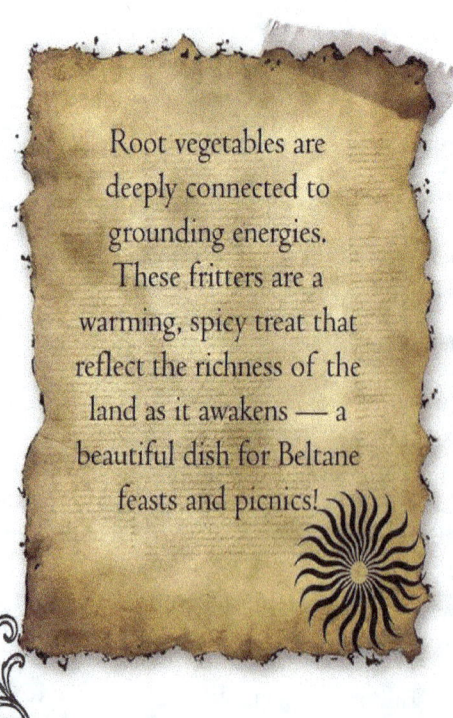

Root vegetables are deeply connected to grounding energies. These fritters are a warming, spicy treat that reflect the richness of the land as it awakens — a beautiful dish for Beltane feasts and picnics!

Spring Greens Salad
with Edible Flowers

Ingredients

- 2 cups mixed spring greens (such as baby spinach, lamb's lettuce, sorrel, or pea shoots)
- 1/2 cup thinly sliced cucumber
- 1/2 cup radishes, thinly sliced
- 1/4 cup fresh herbs (such as dill, mint, or chives), chopped
- 1/4 cup crumbled goat cheese or feta (optional)
- A handful of edible flowers (like nasturtiums, violets, calendula petals, or borage)
- 2 tbsp toasted seeds or nuts (sunflower seeds, pumpkin seeds, or slivered almonds)

For the Dressing:
- 2 tbsp olive oil
- 1 tbsp lemon juice
- 1 tsp honey or maple syrup
- 1/2 tsp Dijon mustard
- Salt & pepper, to taste

Method

1. Rinse and gently pat dry your spring greens and edible flowers.
2. In a large bowl, toss together greens, cucumber, radish, and chopped herbs.
3. In a small jar or bowl, whisk together the olive oil, lemon juice, honey, mustard, salt, and pepper until well combined.
4. Drizzle the dressing over the salad and toss lightly to coat.
5. Sprinkle with cheese (if using), toasted seeds or nuts, and finish with a flourish of edible flowers on top.
6. Serve immediately as a light lunch or as a vibrant side for your Beltane feasting table.

This salad is a celebration of renewal and fresh beginnings — perfect for spring rituals and garden gatherings. Edible flowers not only enchant the eye but carry delicate magic: violets for love, nasturtiums for courage, and borage for joy. Bless your greens and eat with intention.

Spring Vegetable Risotto

Ingredients

- 1 tbsp olive oil or butter
- 1 small onion or shallot, finely chopped
- 2 garlic cloves, minced
- 1 cup arborio rice
- 1/2 cup dry white wine (or extra stock)
- 4 cups hot vegetable stock, kept warm
- 1 cup peas (fresh or frozen)
- 1 cup chopped spring greens (spinach, baby kale, or wild greens)
- Zest of 1 lemon
- 2 tbsp lemon juice
- 2 tbsp fresh herbs (parsley, mint, or dill), chopped
- Salt & pepper, to taste
- Optional: 1/4 cup grated Parmesan or plant-based cheese alternative
- Optional: a spoonful of cream or vegan cream for extra richness

Method

1. Heat oil or butter in a large saucepan over medium heat. Sauté onion until soft and translucent, about 5 minutes.
2. Add garlic and cook for 1 minute more. Stir in the arborio rice and toast for 1–2 minutes, until edges look slightly translucent.
3. Pour in the wine and stir until absorbed.
4. Begin adding warm stock, 1 ladle at a time, stirring often. Wait until the liquid is mostly absorbed before adding more. This will take about 18–20 minutes.
5. When the rice is tender and creamy, stir in peas and greens. Cook for 3–4 minutes until just wilted.
6. Add lemon zest, juice, herbs, salt, pepper, and cheese or cream if using. Stir until luscious and well combined.
7. Serve immediately, garnished with extra herbs or lemon curls.

> This dish sings with the energy of Ostara and Beltane — bright, green, and alive. Peas and spring greens bring renewal, lemon lifts the spirit, and creamy rice brings comfort and balance. Stir with love and intention — each circle of the spoon calls in light, joy, and the lushness of spring.

Stuffed Portobello Mushrooms
with herbed grains & pine nuts – vegan

Ingredients
- 4 large Portobello mushrooms, stems removed and gills gently scraped
- 1 tbsp olive oil
- Salt & pepper, to taste

For the Filling:
- 1/2 cup cooked grains (quinoa, brown rice, or couscous work beautifully)
- 1 small red onion, finely chopped
- 2 garlic cloves, minced
- 1 tbsp olive oil
- 1 tbsp lemon juice
- 2 tbsp fresh parsley, chopped
- 1 tbsp fresh thyme or oregano, chopped (or 1 tsp dried)
- 2 tbsp pine nuts, lightly toasted
- Salt & pepper, to taste

Optional Garnish:
- Nutritional yeast or vegan cheese, for a savoury finish
- Extra herbs or lemon zest

Method

1. Preheat oven to 190°C (375°F). Brush mushrooms with olive oil, season with salt and pepper, and place on a baking tray lined with parchment.
2. In a frying pan, heat olive oil over medium heat. Sauté onion for 3–4 minutes until softened. Add garlic and cook for 1 minute more.
3. Stir in the cooked grains, lemon juice, herbs, pine nuts, salt, and pepper. Cook for another 2 minutes to warm through and combine flavours.
4. Spoon the mixture generously into the mushroom caps.
5. Bake for 20–25 minutes, or until the mushrooms are tender and the tops slightly golden.
6. Sprinkle with nutritional yeast or vegan cheese if using, and finish with fresh herbs or

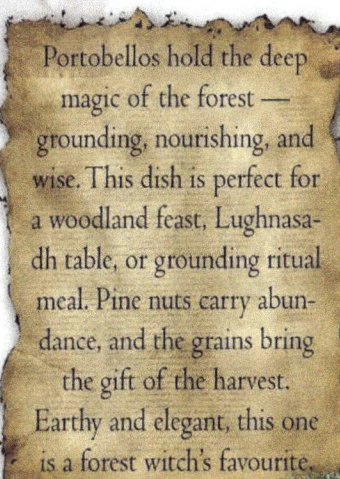

Portobellos hold the deep magic of the forest — grounding, nourishing, and wise. This dish is perfect for a woodland feast, Lughnasadh table, or grounding ritual meal. Pine nuts carry abundance, and the grains bring the gift of the harvest. Earthy and elegant, this one is a forest witch's favourite.

Elderflower Jelly
with Wild Berries

Ingredients

- 500ml (2 cups) elderflower cordial
- 300ml (1 1/4 cups) water
- Juice of 1 lemon
- 2 tbsp sugar (optional, to taste)
- 4–5 gelatine leaves or 2 1/2 tsp powdered gelatine (use agar-agar for vegan)
- 1 cup fresh wild berries (e.g. raspberries, blackberries, bilberries, or strawberries, halved if large)
- Edible flowers or fresh mint, to decorate (optional)

Method

1. If using gelatine leaves, soak them in cold water for 5–10 minutes until soft. If using powdered gelatine, sprinkle over 2 tbsp cold water and let bloom.
2. In a saucepan, gently heat the elderflower cordial, water, lemon juice, and sugar until warm (don't boil).
3. Remove from heat. Stir in softened gelatine (squeeze out excess water first) or the bloomed powder. Stir until fully dissolved.
4. Allow mixture to cool slightly, then pour into individual moulds or a large glass bowl.
5. Drop a handful of wild berries into each jelly. Chill in the fridge for 4–6 hours, or until fully set.
6. To serve, unmould or spoon into dishes. Garnish with extra berries and edible flowers for a magical finish.

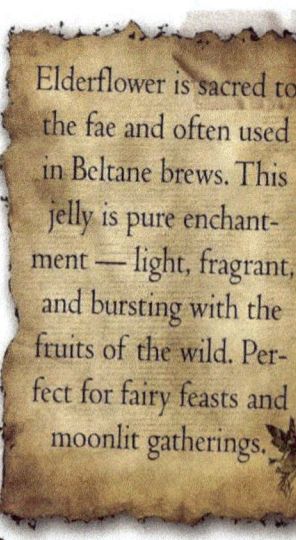

Elderflower is sacred to the fae and often used in Beltane brews. This jelly is pure enchantment — light, fragrant, and bursting with the fruits of the wild. Perfect for fairy feasts and moonlit gatherings.

Honey-Rose Shortbread Biscuits

Ingredients

- 1 cup (227 g) unsalted butter, room temp
- ¼ cup honey (gives it a soft floral sweetness)
- 1/3 cup (66 g) granulated sugar
- 2 1/3 cups (292 g) all-purpose flour
- ½ tsp vanilla extract
- ¾ tsp rose water
- ¼ tsp salt
- 3 tbsp dried rose petals (culinary grade)
- 3 tbsp heavy cream
- 1 cup white chocolate, melted (optional for dipping or drizzling)
- 1 tbsp dried rose petals, lightly crushed (for garnish)
- 1 tbsp pistachios, finely chopped (for garnish—optional, but gives color and crunch)

Method

1. In a large bowl, cream the butter, honey, and sugar until light and fluffy.
2. Add the vanilla and rose water. Mix well.
3. Slowly mix in the flour and salt until just combined.
4. Add the rose petals and cream, stirring until the dough forms a soft ball.
5. Roll out the dough to ¼" thick and cut into desired shapes (flowers, hearts, or circles work well).
6. Chill for 20 minutes (helps them hold shape).
7. Bake at 325°F (165°C) for 12–15 minutes, or until edges are just barely golden.
8. Cool completely. Dip or drizzle with melted white chocolate, then sprinkle with rose petals and pistachios.
9. Let set and store in an airtight container—or serve on your Beltane altar.

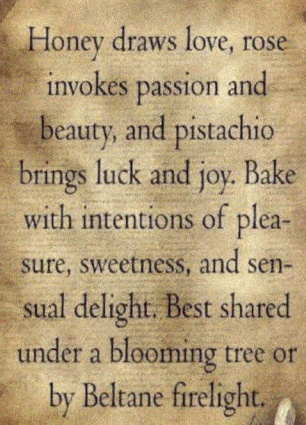

Honey draws love, rose invokes passion and beauty, and pistachio brings luck and joy. Bake with intentions of pleasure, sweetness, and sensual delight. Best shared under a blooming tree or by Beltane firelight.

Maypole Parfait Cups

Ingredients
(Serves 4)

- 2 cups thick Greek-style yogurt (or coconut yogurt for dairy-free)
- 1 tbsp honey or maple syrup (optional, to sweeten yogurt)
- 2 cups granola (your favourite kind – nutty, seedy, or floral)
- 2 cups mixed vibrant fruits (think strawberries, blueberries, mango, kiwi, raspberries, etc.)
- Optional: edible flowers, mint leaves, or a swirl of berry compote to top

These cheerful parfaits reflect the joyful spirals of the Maypole — each colourful layer symbolising growth, fertility, and delight. A fresh, nourishing treat to welcome the warm sun and the abundance it brings.

Method

1. If desired, mix honey or syrup into yogurt for sweetness.
2. In glasses or jars, begin layering: a spoonful of granola, then a dollop of yogurt, followed by a scattering of fruit.
3. Repeat layers until glasses are full, ending with fruit on top.
4. Garnish with edible flowers, fresh mint, or a drizzle of berry compote.
5. Serve immediately, or chill briefly for a cool treat.

Rhubarb & Vanilla Crumble
tangy-sweet fruit with golden, buttery topping

Ingredients
(Serves 4–6)

For the filling:
- 500g (about 4 cups) rhubarb, trimmed and chopped into 2–3cm chunks
- 100g (1/2 cup) caster sugar (adjust to taste)
- 1 tsp vanilla extract or seeds from 1 vanilla pod
- Zest of 1 orange (optional, for brightness)
- 1 tbsp plain flour or cornflour (for thickening)

For the crumble topping:
- 125g (1 cup) plain flour
- 100g (1/2 cup) brown sugar
- 100g (7 tbsp) cold butter, cubed (or plant-based alternative)
- Pinch of salt
- Optional: 2 tbsp chopped hazelnuts, oats, or flaked almonds for texture

Method

1. Preheat oven to 180°C (350°F).
2. In a bowl, toss chopped rhubarb with sugar, vanilla, orange zest (if using), and flour. Spoon into a baking dish.
3. For the crumble, rub butter into the flour with fingertips until it resembles coarse breadcrumbs. Stir in sugar and optional extras.
4. Scatter crumble evenly over the fruit.
5. Bake for 35–40 minutes, or until topping is golden and rhubarb is bubbling at the edges.
6. Serve warm with cream, custard, or a scoop of vanilla ice cream.

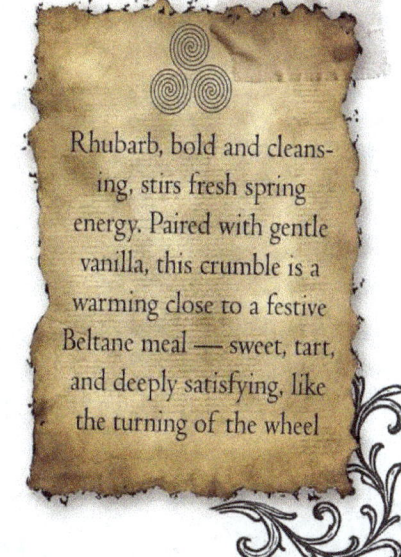

Rhubarb, bold and cleansing, stirs fresh spring energy. Paired with gentle vanilla, this crumble is a warming close to a festive Beltane meal — sweet, tart, and deeply satisfying, like the turning of the wheel

Strawberries & Cream Fairy Cakes

Ingredients
(Makes 12 fairy cakes)
For the cakes:
- 125g (1/2 cup) unsalted butter, softened
- 125g (1/2 cup) caster sugar
- 2 eggs
- 1 tsp vanilla extract
- 125g (1 cup) self-raising flour
- 1–2 tbsp milk, if needed
- 4–5 ripe strawberries, finely chopped

For the frosting:
- 100g (1/2 cup) unsalted butter, softened
- 200g (1 1/2 cups) icing sugar
- 2 tbsp double cream or plant-based cream
- 1–2 tsp rosewater or elderflower cordial (optional, for floral note)
- A few drops of pink natural food dye or beet juice (optional)

Decoration:
- Halved strawberries or dried strawberry slices
- Edible flowers (violas, rose petals, chamomile, etc.)

Method

1. Preheat oven to 180°C (350°F). Line a muffin tin with fairy cake or cupcake cases.
2. Cream butter and sugar together until light and fluffy.
3. Beat in the eggs one at a time, then stir in vanilla.
4. Fold in flour gently, adding a splash of milk if needed to loosen the batter.
5. Fold in the chopped strawberries last, taking care not to overmix.
6. Divide the mixture evenly between cases. Bake for 15–18 minutes, or until golden and springy to the touch. Cool completely before frosting.
7. For the frosting, beat butter until creamy. Gradually add icing sugar, then the cream and rosewater. Beat until fluffy. Add color if desired.
8. Pipe or swirl onto cooled cakes. Decorate with berries and edible blooms.

These fairy cakes sing of springtime joy and Beltane sweetness — a perfect offering for nature spirits or a treat to share at garden picnics. Strawberries stir the heart, and flowers invite beauty and blessing into every bite.

Beltane Blossom Fizz
(Non-alcoholic)

Ingredients

- 1 cup elderflower cordial (store-bought or homemade)
- 2 cups sparkling water or club soda
- 1/2 cup mixed berries (fresh or frozen: raspberries, blueberries, strawberries)
- A few edible flower petals (violas, pansies, rose, etc.)
- Ice cubes
- Fresh mint for garnish

Method

1. In a pitcher, gently muddle the berries.
2. Add ice cubes, elderflower cordial, and sparkling water. Stir gently.
3. Pour into glasses and float edible petals and mint on top.
4. Optional: Rim glasses with sugar and a hint of lemon zest for extra charm.

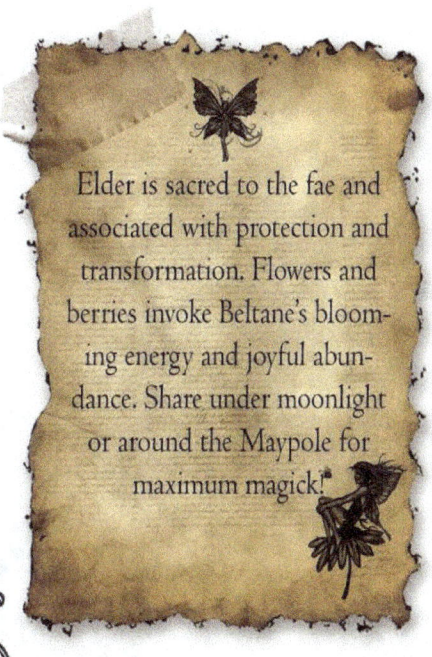

Elder is sacred to the fae and associated with protection and transformation. Flowers and berries invoke Beltane's blooming energy and joyful abundance. Share under moonlight or around the Maypole for maximum magick!

Hawthorn Cordial
a fragrant heart tonic steeped in Beltane magic

Ingredients
(Makes approx. 500ml)

- 2 cups fresh hawthorn blossoms (or 1 cup dried)
- 500ml (2 cups) water
- 200g (1 cup) sugar (or honey, to taste)
- Juice of 1 lemon
- Optional: A strip of lemon zest or a few rose petals for extra heart-opening vibes

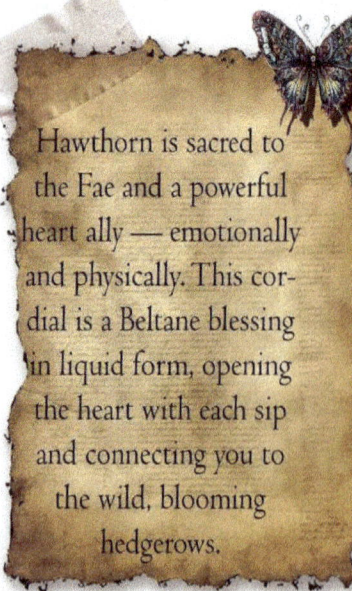

Hawthorn is sacred to the Fae and a powerful heart ally — emotionally and physically. This cordial is a Beltane blessing in liquid form, opening the heart with each sip and connecting you to the wild, blooming hedgerows.

To Serve:
Mix with sparkling water, still water, or drizzle into herbal tea. Try it over ice with mint and berries, or add a splash to a cocktail for some floral enchantment.

Method
1. Gently rinse the fresh blossoms to remove any insects.
2. In a saucepan, bring water to a gentle simmer. Add the hawthorn blossoms and any optional additions.
3. Remove from heat, cover, and let steep for 30–60 minutes. For stronger flavour, let steep longer or overnight.
4. Strain the liquid into a clean pan. Add sugar or honey and stir over low heat until dissolved.
5. Add lemon juice, then pour into sterilised bottles. Store in the fridge and use within 2–3 weeks. For longer storage, freeze in portions.

Meadow Mead Spritz
effervescent with lemon balm & citrus

Ingredients
(Serves 2)

- 250ml (1 cup) sparkling mead (chilled)
- A small handful of fresh lemon balm leaves
- Juice of 1/2 an orange
- Juice of 1/2 a lemon
- 150ml (about 2/3 cup) sparkling water or soda water
- Thin slices of lemon and orange, for garnish
- Ice cubes
- Optional: a touch of honey or elderflower syrup for extra sweetness

Method

1. Lightly muddle the lemon balm leaves in the bottom of a jug or shaker to release their aroma.
2. Add orange and lemon juice, and honey or syrup if using. Stir gently to combine.
3. Add ice, then pour in the mead and sparkling water. Stir just once or twice to mix — don't lose the bubbles!
4. Pour into glasses, garnish with citrus slices and a lemon balm sprig.

This spritz is summer in a sip. Lemon balm uplifts the mood, while mead — ancient and golden — carries Beltane joy and a gentle warmth from the bees. Sip to celebrate love, life, and everything blooming.

To Serve:
Serve immediately, preferably outside with bare feet and laughter nearby.

Strawberry-Mint Beltane Cooler

Ingredients
(Serves 2)
- 1 cup (150g) fresh strawberries, hulled and sliced
- A handful of fresh mint leaves (plus extra for garnish)
- 1 tbsp lemon juice
- 1 tbsp honey or maple syrup (adjust to taste)
- 300ml (1¼ cups) chilled still or sparkling water
- Ice cubes
- Optional: splash of elderflower cordial or a dash of rosewater

Method
1. In a jug or blender, muddle or blitz the strawberries and mint until juicy and fragrant.
2. Strain if you'd prefer a smooth cooler, or leave rustic with the pulp for extra flavour.
3. Stir in lemon juice and honey until well mixed.
4. Add ice and top up with still or sparkling water.
5. Pour into glasses and garnish with mint sprigs and a sliced strawberry on the rim.

Strawberries carry the sweetness of love and new beginnings, while mint clears the mind and uplifts the spirit. This Beltane brew is perfect for toasting fertility, creativity, and joyous connection.

To Serve:
Best sipped in the shade of a blooming tree, with petals falling around you and laughter echoing through the fields.

Beltane Fire Butter

Ingredients

- 125g (1/2 cup) unsalted butter (or vegan butter), softened
- 1 small garlic clove, finely minced
- 1/2 tsp smoked paprika
- 1/4 tsp ground cayenne pepper (adjust to taste)
- Zest of 1/2 lemon
- 1 tsp chopped fresh thyme or rosemary
- A pinch of sea salt
- Optional: a tiny drizzle of honey for balance

Method

1. In a small bowl, mix all ingredients together until smooth and evenly combined.
2. Taste and adjust the heat level — add more cayenne for extra fire, or a touch more lemon zest for brightness.
3. Spoon onto a sheet of baking paper or cling film and roll into a log, or press into a jar or ramekin.
4. Chill until firm, or serve soft at room temperature.

This butter channels the crackling energy of Beltane fires — passion, transformation, and vitality. With heat from cayenne and grounding herbs, it's a perfect offering to the flame or a spicy finish to your feast.

To Use:
Dollop onto warm bread, roast veggies, grilled corn, or melt over fire-roasted meats. Also lovely stirred into rice or couscous for a fiery kick.

Dandelion Jelly

Ingredients

- 4 cups fresh dandelion petals (yellow parts only, no green bits)
- 4 cups water
- 1 tbsp lemon juice
- Zest of 1 small lemon
- 1 apple, grated (adds natural pectin)
- 3 cups granulated sugar (or to taste)
- 1 packet pectin

Method

1. Gently rinse dandelion petals to remove bugs or dirt. Place in a saucepan with water, grated apple, and lemon zest.
2. Bring to a boil, then simmer gently for 30 minutes. Remove from heat, cover, and let steep 6 hours or overnight.
3. Strain through muslin or a fine sieve, squeezing out every drop of golden infusion.
4. Return the liquid to the pan. Stir in lemon juice and pectin. Bring to a rolling boil.
5. Add sugar, stirring constantly. Boil hard for 1–2 minutes or until it begins to set (check using a chilled spoon).
6. Pour into sterilised jars and seal while hot. Let cool at room temperature.

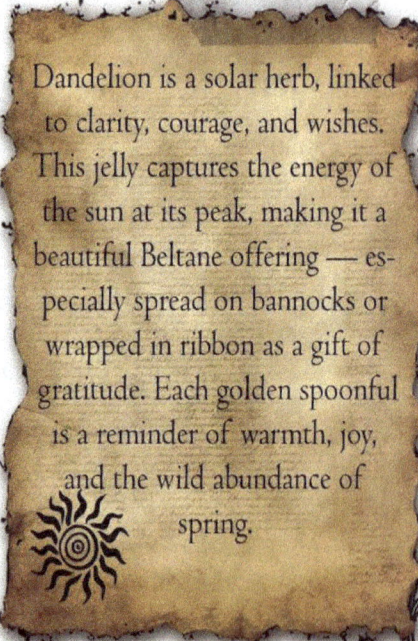

Dandelion is a solar herb, linked to clarity, courage, and wishes. This jelly captures the energy of the sun at its peak, making it a beautiful Beltane offering — especially spread on bannocks or wrapped in ribbon as a gift of gratitude. Each golden spoonful is a reminder of warmth, joy, and the wild abundance of spring.

Samhain: A Feast Beyond the Veil

Samhain (pronounced sow-in) marks one of the most sacred points on the Wheel of the Year — the witch's new year and a powerful festival of endings, beginnings, and remembrance. Celebrated from October 31st through November 1st, Samhain signals the final harvest, the darkening of the year, and the time when the veil between worlds is at its thinnest.

Rooted in ancient Celtic tradition, Samhain was the dividing line between summer's light and winter's darkness. Fires were lit, animals were culled, and offerings were made to honour ancestors and appease wandering spirits. It is a night of divination, shadow work, and deep spiritual reflection — but also of comfort, gathering, and shared warmth.

Food lies at the very heart of Samhain, carrying both symbolic weight and practical comfort. Traditional dishes often include final harvest fruits, roots, nuts, grains, and preserved goods. Breads and cakes were baked as offerings for the dead, while stews and hearty fare nourished the living against the coming cold. Sweet treats honour beloved spirits and children alike, echoing the ancient practice of leaving food at thresholds to welcome or ward off the unseen.

In this Samhain recipe collection, each dish is a ritual of its own — a spell woven from earth's last bounty, a remembrance of kin, a celebration of cyclical change. Whether you're baking soul cakes, simmering cider, or wrapping gifts for ancestral altars, may these recipes nourish your body, spirit, and sacred connection to the turning year.

Litha Invocation
To Call in the Light of the Sun

O radiant Sun, at your height and power,
We greet you on this longest day.
Shine upon us with golden grace,
And awaken the fire within.
Spirits of Summer, dance through leaf and bloom,
Fill our hearts with warmth, laughter, and life.
Bless this sacred season of ripening,
Where dreams blossom beneath clear skies.
We call upon the light of Litha—
The flame of passion, the joy of growth,
The magic of herbs, the sweetness of fruit,
The sacred turning of the Wheel.
May this moment be held in sun-drenched stillness,
And may all we plant—within and without—
Come forth in beauty and in bounty.
So mote it be.

Litha Blessing

May the golden sun warm your spirit,
May the ripe earth fill your hands.
May your table be rich with the season's gifts,
And your heart be full of laughter and light.
May flowers bloom along your path,
And herbs whisper secrets in the breeze.
May joy rise like midsummer fire,
And love shine like the longest day.
Blessed be this Solstice hour—
A turning point, a celebration,
A feast for the soul and the senses.
Blessed Litha

Sun Wheel Braided Bread

Ingredients (Makes 1 large loaf)

- 3½ cups plain (all-purpose) flour
- 1 tbsp sugar
- 1 tsp salt
- 2¼ tsp active dry yeast (1 packet)
- 1 cup warm water
- 2 tbsp olive oil
- 1 egg (for egg wash, optional)
- Optional: fresh rosemary, thyme, or edible flowers for garnish

---

Braiding bread in a wheel shape honors the turning of the sun at Litha. Each strand woven into the whole reflects unity, cycles, and abundance. A perfect centrepiece for your sabbat feast—best served warm with herbed butter or honey.

Method

1. In a bowl, mix warm water, sugar, and yeast. Let sit for 5–10 minutes until frothy.
2. Add flour, salt, and olive oil. Knead for 8–10 minutes until smooth and elastic.
3. Cover and let rise in a warm spot for 1 hour or until doubled.
4. Divide dough into 3 strands, braid into a circle or spiral wheel shape. Tuck ends together.
5. Place on a baking sheet. Cover and let rise again for 30 minutes.
6. Preheat oven to 375°F (190°C). Brush with beaten egg if using. Add herbs or flowers for decoration.
7. Bake for 25–30 minutes or until golden brown. Cool slightly before serving.

Honey Oat Harvest Loaf

Ingredients
(Makes 1 loaf)

- 1 cup rolled oats
- 1 1/3 cups boiling water
- 2 tbsp honey (or maple syrup)
- 2¼ tsp active dry yeast
- 2 tbsp butter or vegan butter, melted
- 1½ tsp salt
- 2½ to 3 cups all-purpose or bread flour
- Extra oats for topping

Method

1. In a large bowl, pour boiling water over oats. Stir in honey and let sit until lukewarm (about 15–20 minutes).
2. Stir in yeast and let stand for 5–10 minutes, until foamy.
3. Add melted butter and salt. Mix in flour, ½ cup at a time, until a soft dough forms.
4. Knead on a floured surface for about 8 minutes, until smooth and elastic.
5. Place dough in a greased bowl, cover, and let rise in a warm spot for about 1 hour, or until doubled.
6. Punch down and shape into a loaf. Place in a greased loaf pan, cover, and rise again for 30–40 minutes.
7. Preheat oven to 350°F (175°C). Brush top with water or plant milk and sprinkle with oats.
8. Bake for 35–40 minutes, or until golden and hollow-sounding. Let cool completely before slicing.

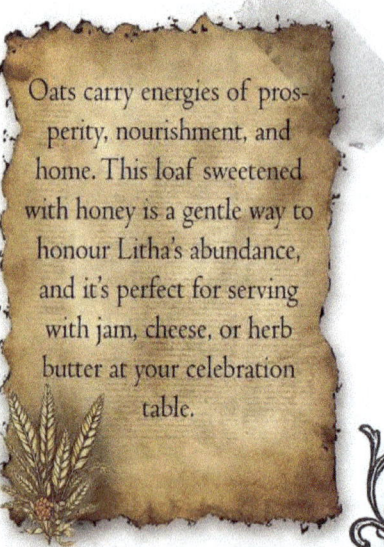

Oats carry energies of prosperity, nourishment, and home. This loaf sweetened with honey is a gentle way to honour Litha's abundance, and it's perfect for serving with jam, cheese, or herb butter at your celebration table.

Lemon Verbena Shortbread Cookies

Ingredients
(Makes about 20 small cookies)
- 1 cup (225g) unsalted butter or vegan butter, softened
- ½ cup (100g) sugar
- 2 cups (250g) all-purpose flour
- 1 tbsp finely chopped fresh lemon verbena leaves (or 1 tsp dried)
- Zest of 1 lemon
- Pinch of salt

Method

1. Cream butter and sugar together until light and fluffy.
2. Add lemon zest, chopped lemon verbena, and salt. Stir to combine.
3. Mix in flour until dough forms. Shape into a log, wrap in parchment or cling film, and chill for at least 1 hour.
4. Preheat oven to 325°F (160°C). Slice chilled dough into ¼-inch rounds and place on a lined baking sheet.
5. Bake for 12–15 minutes, or until edges are just golden. Let cool on a wire rack.

Lemon verbena lifts the spirit and enhances clarity—perfect for midsummer spells or simply tuning into joy. These melt-in-your-mouth cookies carry the brightness of the season in each bite and pair beautifully with a sunny herbal tea or a sunset walk.

Litha Herb & Flower Focaccia

Ingredients
(Makes 1 tray-bake loaf)

- 2¼ tsp instant yeast
- 1½ cups warm water
- 1 tsp sugar
- 3½ cups all-purpose flour
- 1½ tsp salt
- ¼ cup olive oil (plus more for drizzling)
- Fresh herbs (rosemary, thyme, oregano)
- Edible flowers (nasturtiums, violets, calendula, or pansies)
- Flaky sea salt

Method

1. In a bowl, dissolve yeast and sugar in warm water. Let sit until frothy (about 5–10 minutes).
2. Stir in flour, salt, and olive oil. Mix to form a sticky dough.
3. Knead lightly on a floured surface, then transfer to a lightly oiled bowl. Cover and rise for 1–1½ hours.
4. Punch down and press into a greased or parchment-lined baking tray. Dimple the surface with your fingertips.
5. Drizzle with olive oil, press herbs and edible flowers gently into the dough, and sprinkle with flaky salt.
6. Let rise again for 30 minutes. Meanwhile, preheat oven to 400°F (200°C).
7. Bake for 20–25 minutes, or until golden brown. Cool slightly before slicing.

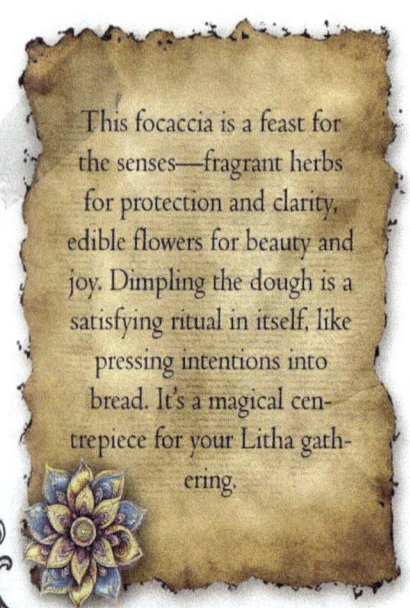

This focaccia is a feast for the senses—fragrant herbs for protection and clarity, edible flowers for beauty and joy. Dimpling the dough is a satisfying ritual in itself, like pressing intentions into bread. It's a magical centerpiece for your Litha gathering.

Rosemary & Olive Sun Bread

Ingredients
(Makes 1 round loaf)

- 3 cups all-purpose or bread flour
- 2¼ tsp instant yeast
- 1 tsp sugar
- 1 tsp salt
- 1¼ cups warm water
- 2 tbsp olive oil (plus extra for brushing)
- ½ cup chopped mixed olives
- 1 tbsp chopped fresh rosemary
- Optional: flaky sea salt for topping

Method

1. In a large bowl, mix flour, yeast, sugar, and salt. Add warm water and olive oil. Stir to form a rough dough.
2. Knead for 8–10 minutes until smooth. Add olives and rosemary and knead gently to incorporate.
3. Place in a lightly oiled bowl, cover, and let rise in a warm place for 1 hour, or until doubled in size.
4. Punch down dough and shape into a round. Place on a parchment-lined baking sheet. Score a sunburst pattern on top with a sharp knife or scissors.
5. Cover and let rise for 30–40 minutes. Preheat oven to 375°F (190°C).
6. Brush with olive oil and sprinkle with flaky salt if using. Bake for 30–35 minutes, or until golden and hollow-sounding when tapped. Cool on a wire rack.

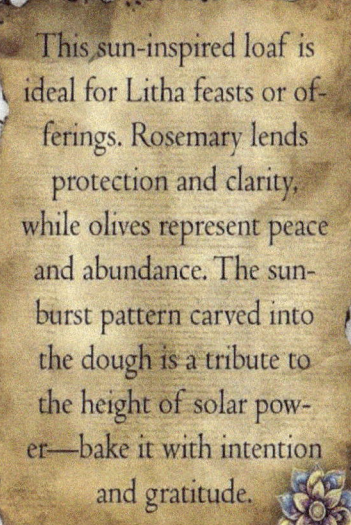

This sun-inspired loaf is ideal for Litha feasts or offerings. Rosemary lends protection and clarity, while olives represent peace and abundance. The sunburst pattern carved into the dough is a tribute to the height of solar power—bake it with intention and gratitude.

Golden Litha Honey Cake

Ingredients
(Serves 8–10)

- 1½ cups all-purpose flour
- 1 tsp baking powder
- ½ tsp baking soda
- ½ tsp cinnamon
- ¼ tsp salt
- 2 large eggs
- ½ cup plain Greek yogurt (or plant-based yogurt)
- ½ cup unsalted butter, melted (or neutral oil for dairy-free)
- ¾ cup honey
- ¼ cup brown sugar
- 1 tsp vanilla extract
- Zest of 1 lemon (optional for brightness)

Optional glaze:
- 2 tbsp honey
- 1 tbsp lemon juice

Method

1. Preheat oven to 175°C (350°F). Grease and line a small round or loaf cake tin.
2. In a bowl, whisk together flour, baking powder, baking soda, cinnamon, and salt.
3. In a separate bowl, beat eggs with yogurt, melted butter, honey, brown sugar, vanilla, and lemon zest until smooth.
4. Fold the dry ingredients into the wet until just combined—don't overmix.
5. Pour into the prepared tin and bake for 35–40 minutes, or until golden and a skewer comes out clean.
6. While warm, drizzle with the optional honey-lemon glaze for extra shine and zing.

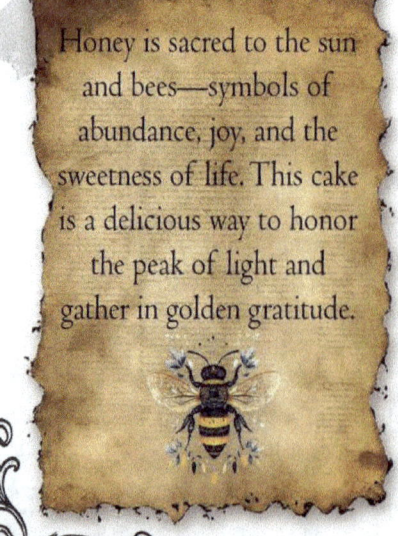

Honey is sacred to the sun and bees—symbols of abundance, joy, and the sweetness of life. This cake is a delicious way to honor the peak of light and gather in golden gratitude.

Grilled Vegetable Skewers
with Lemon-Herb Marinade

Ingredients
(Serves 4)
- 1 red bell pepper, cut into chunks
- 1 yellow bell pepper, cut into chunks
- 1 zucchini, sliced into thick rounds
- 1 red onion, cut into wedges
- 8–10 cherry tomatoes
- 1 small eggplant, cut into cubes
- Wooden or metal skewers (if using wooden, soak in water for 30 mins first)

For the Marinade:
- ¼ cup olive oil
- Juice and zest of 1 lemon
- 2 cloves garlic, minced
- 1 tbsp fresh thyme leaves
- 1 tbsp fresh rosemary, finely chopped
- Salt and pepper to taste

Method
1. Combine all marinade ingredients in a bowl or jar and whisk to blend.
2. Thread vegetables onto skewers, alternating colors and shapes for a festive look.
3. Place skewers in a shallow dish or tray and pour marinade over them. Turn to coat evenly. Let sit for at least 30 minutes (or cover and refrigerate for up to 4 hours).
4. Preheat grill or grill pan over medium heat. Grill skewers for 10–12 minutes, turning occasionally, until vegetables are tender and slightly charred.
5. Serve hot, garnished with fresh herbs or a final squeeze of lemon.

These colourful skewers celebrate the vibrant bounty of the summer garden. The lemon and herbs invoke cleansing and protection, while the flame-grilled veggies honour Litha's solar fire. A radiant offering for your sabbat table or midsummer picnic.

Herbed Goat Cheese & Edible Flower Crostini

Ingredients
(Makes about 12 crostini)

- 1 baguette, sliced into 12 rounds
- Olive oil for brushing
- 150g (5 oz) soft goat cheese (or plant-based alternative)
- 1 tsp lemon zest
- 1 tbsp chopped fresh herbs (thyme, basil, or chives work beautifully)
- Salt & pepper to taste
- Edible flowers (nasturtiums, violets, pansies, borage, or calendula petals)

Method

1. Preheat oven to 375°F (190°C). Arrange baguette slices on a baking sheet and lightly brush with olive oil.
2. Toast for 8–10 minutes until golden and crisp. Let cool slightly.
3. In a bowl, mix goat cheese with lemon zest, herbs, salt, and pepper.
4. Spread a generous layer of herbed cheese onto each crostini.
5. Garnish with a few petals or a whole edible flower for each. Serve immediately.

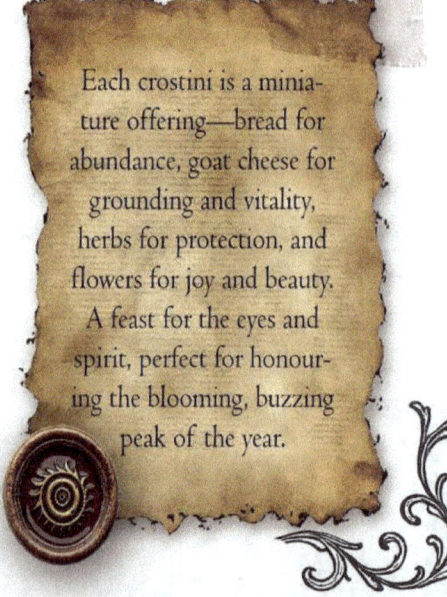

Each crostini is a miniature offering—bread for abundance, goat cheese for grounding and vitality, herbs for protection, and flowers for joy and beauty. A feast for the eyes and spirit, perfect for honouring the blooming, buzzing peak of the year.

Lemon Balm & Honey Glazed Chicken Thighs

Ingredients
(Serves 4)

- 4 bone-in, skin-on chicken thighs
- 2 tbsp fresh lemon balm leaves, finely chopped
- Zest and juice of 1 lemon
- 2 tbsp honey
- 2 cloves garlic, minced
- 1 tbsp olive oil
- ½ tsp salt
- ¼ tsp black pepper

Lemon balm, sacred to the bee and long used for love and joy magic, brings sunny brightness to this dish. As the sun reaches its peak at Litha, this herb helps uplift the spirit and heart. Serve this under open skies if you can, and let the golden glaze honour the golden day.

Method

1. Preheat oven to 200°C (400°F). Line a baking tray with parchment paper.
2. In a small bowl, whisk together lemon balm, lemon zest and juice, honey, garlic, olive oil, salt, and pepper.
3. Pat chicken thighs dry and place on the tray. Brush generously with the glaze.
4. Roast for 35–40 minutes, basting once or twice with remaining glaze, until the chicken is golden and cooked through.

Litha Herb-Crusted Salmon
with Citrus Butter

Ingredients
(Serves 4)

- 4 salmon fillets, skin-on
- Zest of 1 orange
- Zest of 1 lemon
- 2 tbsp fresh dill, chopped
- 1 tbsp fresh thyme leaves
- 1 tbsp parsley, chopped
- 2 tbsp breadcrumbs (or ground seeds/nuts for gluten-free)
- Salt and pepper to taste
- 2 tbsp butter (or vegan butter)
- Juice of ½ orange and ½ lemon

Method

1. Preheat oven to 400°F (200°C). Line a baking tray with parchment or foil.
2. In a bowl, mix orange and lemon zest, dill, thyme, parsley, and breadcrumbs. Season with salt and pepper.
3. Place salmon fillets on the tray, skin-side down. Press herb mixture onto each fillet, covering the tops.
4. In a small saucepan, melt butter with citrus juice over low heat. Drizzle a little over each fillet.
5. Bake salmon for 12–15 minutes, until flakes easily with a fork.
6. Drizzle with remaining citrus butter before serving.

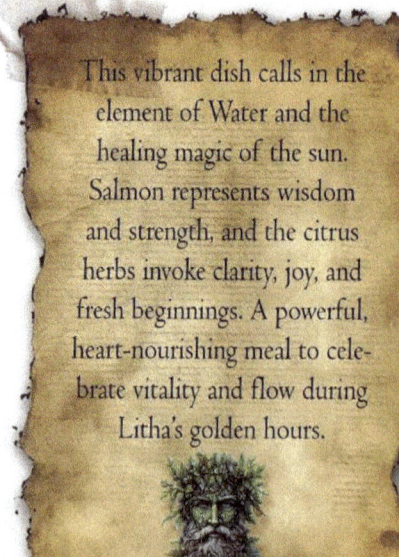

This vibrant dish calls in the element of Water and the healing magic of the sun. Salmon represents wisdom and strength, and the citrus herbs invoke clarity, joy, and fresh beginnings. A powerful, heart-nourishing meal to celebrate vitality and flow during Litha's golden hours.

Mini Spinach & Feta Pastry Twists

Ingredients
(Makes about 16 twists)

- 1 sheet puff pastry (thawed)
- 1 cup baby spinach, finely chopped
- ½ cup crumbled feta (or vegan feta)
- 1 egg, beaten (or plant-based milk for vegan glaze)
- ½ tsp dried oregano
- Salt & pepper to taste
- Sesame seeds or nigella seeds (optional, for topping)

Method

1. Preheat oven to 400°F (200°C). Line a baking tray with parchment paper.
2. In a bowl, mix spinach, feta, oregano, salt, and pepper.
3. Roll out puff pastry and cut in half lengthwise. Spread spinach mixture evenly over one half.
4. Place the other pastry half on top and press gently. Slice into strips (about 1 inch wide), then twist each strip 2–3 times.
5. Place twists on the tray, brush with egg or plant milk, and sprinkle with seeds if using.
6. Bake for 15–18 minutes, until puffed and golden.

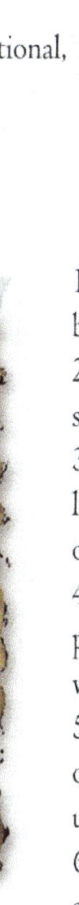

Spinach is a leafy green tied to strength and vitality, while flaky pastry reminds us of transformation—layers upon layers unfolding like the Wheel itself. Perfect picnic fare, these twists pair well with storytelling and a sun-dappled forest glade.

Peach & Honey Midsummer Galette

Ingredients
(Serves 6–8)

For the crust:
- 1¼ cups all-purpose flour
- 1 tbsp sugar
- ¼ tsp salt
- ½ cup cold butter (or vegan butter), cubed
- 3–5 tbsp ice water

For the filling:
- 3–4 ripe peaches, thinly sliced
- 2 tbsp honey (or maple syrup for vegan option)
- 1 tbsp cornstarch
- 1 tsp vanilla extract
- ½ tsp ground cinnamon
- A pinch of nutmeg

To finish:
- 1 egg (or plant milk) for brushing
- Extra honey for drizzling

Method

1. Make the crust: In a bowl, mix flour, sugar, and salt. Cut in cold butter until crumbly. Add ice water 1 tbsp at a time until dough just comes together. Form into a disk, wrap, and chill for 30 minutes.
2. Preheat oven to 375°F (190°C).
3. In another bowl, gently toss peach slices with honey, cornstarch, vanilla, cinnamon, and nutmeg.
4. Roll chilled dough into a rough circle about 12 inches wide. Transfer to a parchment-lined baking sheet.
5. Arrange peach filling in the center, leaving a 2-inch border. Fold edges over the fruit, pleating as you go.
6. Brush crust with egg or plant milk and bake for 35–40 minutes, until golden and bubbling.
7. Drizzle with extra honey while still warm.

> Peaches radiate the energy of love, happiness, and sensuality—just like Litha itself. This rustic galette honours simplicity and beauty, perfect for a solstice picnic or a dreamy fireside feast under the stars.

Savory Summer Herb & Cheese Hand Pies

Ingredients
(Makes about 8 small pies)

For the pastry:
- 2¼ cups all-purpose flour
- ½ tsp salt
- ¾ cup cold butter (or dairy-free shortening), cubed
- 6–8 tbsp cold water

For the filling:
- 1 cup crumbled feta or goat cheese
- ½ cup ricotta or cream cheese
- 2 tbsp chopped fresh parsley
- 1 tbsp chopped fresh chives
- 1 tbsp chopped fresh dill or basil
- Salt & pepper to taste
- Optional: ½ tsp lemon zest for brightness

Method

1. Make the pastry: mix flour and salt, then cut in the butter until crumbly. Add water slowly and bring into a dough. Chill 30 minutes.
2. In a bowl, mix all filling ingredients until smooth.
3. Roll out the pastry and cut into circles or squares (approx. 4–5 inches across).
4. Spoon filling into the center of each, fold over, and crimp the edges with a fork.
5. Bake at 190°C (375°F) for 20–25 minutes, or until golden and crisp.
6. Cool before packing—perfect warm or at room temperature!

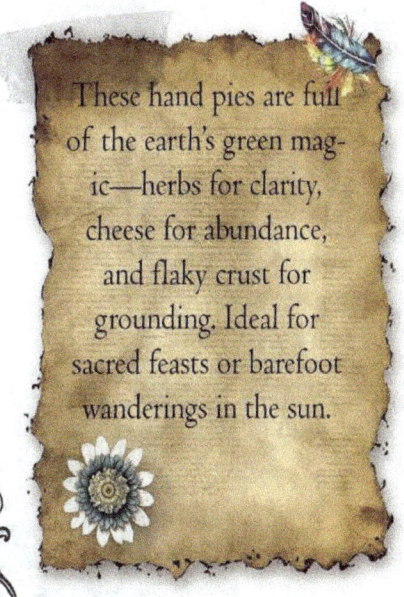

These hand pies are full of the earth's green magic—herbs for clarity, cheese for abundance, and flaky crust for grounding. Ideal for sacred feasts or barefoot wanderings in the sun.

Stuffed Zucchini Boats
with Quinoa and Sun-Dried Tomatoes

Ingredients
(Serves 4)
- 4 medium zucchini
- 1 cup cooked quinoa
- ¼ cup sun-dried tomatoes (oil-packed or rehydrated), chopped
- ½ cup crumbled feta cheese (or vegan feta alternative)
- 2 cloves garlic, minced
- ¼ cup fresh parsley or basil, chopped
- 1 tbsp olive oil
- Salt and pepper to taste
- Optional: pine nuts or toasted seeds for garnish

Method

1. Preheat oven to 350°F (175°C). Line an 8x8-inch baking pan with parchment.
2. In a bowl, mix oats, flour, sugar, cinnamon, and salt. Cut in the butter using a fork or fingers until crumbly.
3. Press two-thirds of the mixture into the prepared pan to form a crust.
4. In another bowl, toss berries with syrup, lemon juice, cornflour, and vanilla if using. Spread over crust.
5. Sprinkle remaining crumble over the top.
6. Bake for 30–35 minutes until topping is golden and berries are bubbling.
7. Cool completely before cutting into bars.

Zucchini boats carry the golden sun of summer in their bright, abundant flesh. With quinoa for strength and sun-dried tomatoes for solar energy, these boats are perfect vessels of nourishment and intention—offering balance, growth, and gratitude at the height of the sun's power.

Summer Garden Pasta
with Roasted Cherry Tomatoes & Basil Pesto

Ingredients
(Serves 4)

- 300g (about 10 oz) spaghetti or pasta of choice
- 2 cups cherry tomatoes
- 1 tbsp olive oil
- Salt and pepper to taste

For the pesto:
- 2 cups fresh basil leaves
- ¼ cup pine nuts (or walnuts)
- 2 cloves garlic
- ½ cup olive oil
- ¼ cup grated Parmesan (or nutritional yeast for vegan version)
- Juice of ½ lemon
- Salt to taste

Optional toppings:
- Extra basil leaves, toasted seeds, edible flowers, or vegan feta

Method

1. Preheat oven to 375°F (190°C). Toss cherry tomatoes with olive oil, salt, and pepper. Roast for 20–25 minutes until softened and slightly caramelized.
2. Meanwhile, cook pasta according to package directions. Drain, reserving a little pasta water.
3. In a food processor or blender, combine all pesto ingredients. Blend until smooth, adjusting salt or lemon to taste.
4. Toss hot pasta with pesto and a splash of pasta water to loosen if needed. Gently fold in roasted tomatoes.
5. Serve warm or at room temperature with your chosen toppings.

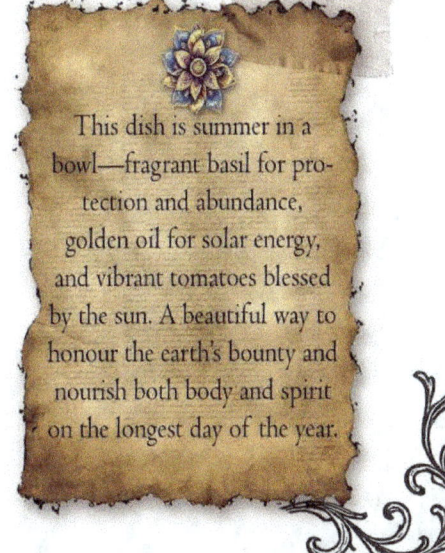

This dish is summer in a bowl—fragrant basil for protection and abundance, golden oil for solar energy, and vibrant tomatoes blessed by the sun. A beautiful way to honour the earth's bounty and nourish both body and spirit on the longest day of the year.

Summer Solstice Corn Fritters
with Spiced Aioli

Ingredients
(Makes about 12 small fritters)
- 1½ cups fresh or thawed corn kernels
- ½ red bell pepper, finely chopped
- 2 spring onions, sliced
- ½ cup flour (or chickpea flour for gluten-free)
- 1 tsp baking powder
- ¼ tsp turmeric
- Salt & pepper to taste
- 2 eggs (or flax eggs for vegan: 2 tbsp flaxseed + 5 tbsp water)
- 2 tbsp milk (or plant milk)
- Oil for frying

For the spiced aioli:
- ½ cup mayonnaise (or vegan mayo)
- 1 garlic clove, minced
- 1 tsp lemon juice
- ½ tsp smoked paprika
- A pinch of cayenne (optional)
- Salt to taste

Method
1. In a large bowl, mix corn, bell pepper, and spring onions.
2. In a separate bowl, whisk together flour, baking powder, turmeric, salt, and pepper. Add eggs and milk, then fold in the veggies.
3. Heat oil in a skillet over medium heat. Drop spoonfuls of the batter into the pan, flattening slightly. Cook 2–3 minutes each side until golden and crisp. Drain on paper towels.
4. Mix all aioli ingredients in a small bowl and chill until ready to serve.
5. Serve fritters warm with a dollop of spiced aioli.

Golden like the Solstice sun, these fritters are a cheerful offering for your Litha table. Corn, sacred in many traditions, is tied to fertility, prosperity, and solar magic. Add a bit of cayenne to your aioli to invoke fiery energy and

Sunshine Stuffed Bell Peppers
with Couscous & Summer Veggies

Ingredients
(Serves 4)

- 4 large bell peppers (red, yellow, or orange)
- 1 cup couscous
- 1¼ cups vegetable broth or hot water
- 1 small zucchini, finely diced
- 1 carrot, grated
- ½ red onion, finely chopped
- ½ cup cherry tomatoes, halved
- 2 tbsp olive oil
- 1 tsp smoked paprika
- 1 tsp dried oregano
- Salt & pepper to taste
- Fresh parsley or mint, to garnish

Method

1. Preheat oven to 375°F (190°C). Slice tops off bell peppers and remove seeds and membranes. Set aside.
2. In a heatproof bowl, pour hot vegetable broth over couscous. Cover and let sit for 5 minutes, then fluff with a fork.
3. Heat olive oil in a pan. Sauté onion, zucchini, and carrot for about 5 minutes until just soft. Add cherry tomatoes, paprika, oregano, salt, and pepper. Cook another 2 minutes.
4. Mix sautéed veggies into couscous. Spoon mixture into bell peppers and place them upright in a baking dish.
5. Cover with foil and bake for 30–35 minutes. Uncover for the last 10 minutes to lightly brown the tops.
6. Garnish with fresh herbs before serving.

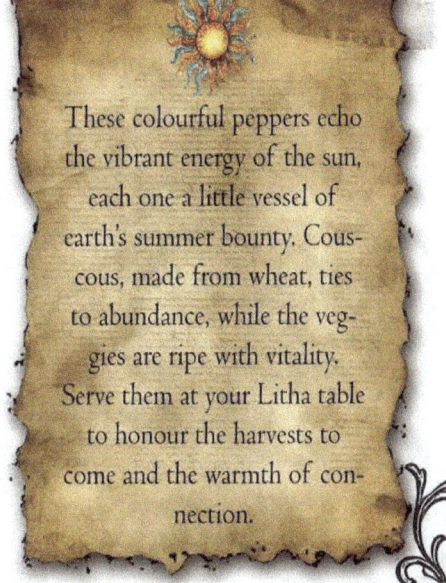

These colourful peppers echo the vibrant energy of the sun, each one a little vessel of earth's summer bounty. Couscous, made from wheat, ties to abundance, while the veggies are ripe with vitality. Serve them at your Litha table to honour the harvests to come and the warmth of connection.

Caramelized Peach & Thyme Tartlets

Ingredients
(Makes 6 mini tartlets or 1 small tart)

For the crust:
- 1¼ cups plain flour
- 1 tbsp sugar
- ¼ tsp salt
- ½ cup cold butter (or dairy-free alternative), cubed
- 2–4 tbsp cold water

For the filling:
- 3 ripe peaches, sliced thinly
- 2 tbsp brown sugar
- 1 tbsp fresh thyme leaves
- 1 tbsp butter (or olive oil for vegan option)
- 1 tsp vanilla extract
- Optional: a splash of lemon juice

Method

1. Make the crust: In a bowl, mix flour, sugar, and salt. Cut in the cold butter until crumbly. Add cold water a spoonful at a time until the dough comes together. Chill for 30 minutes.
2. Roll out and press dough into tartlet pans or a small tart tin. Prick with a fork and bake at 180°C (350°F) for 10 minutes.
3. While crusts bake, gently sauté the peaches in a pan with butter, brown sugar, thyme, vanilla, and lemon juice. Cook until just soft and caramelized.
4. Spoon the peaches into the pre-baked tart shells and bake another 10–15 minutes until bubbling and golden.
5. Cool slightly before serving. Best enjoyed warm or at room temp!

Thyme is said to invite courage, while peaches bring luck and love. Combined with sugar and sun-kissed fire, this tart is a Litha offering fit for fae and feast alike.

Watermelon, Feta & Mint Skewers

Ingredients
(Makes about 20 bite-sized skewers)

- 2 cups seedless watermelon, cut into 1-inch cubes
- 200g (7 oz) feta cheese, cut into 1-inch cubes (or use a vegan feta-style block)
- Fresh mint leaves
- Balsamic glaze (optional)
- Toothpicks or mini skewers

Method

1. Assemble by threading one watermelon cube, one mint leaf (folded if large), and one feta cube onto each skewer or toothpick.
2. Arrange on a platter in a sunburst or spiral for added visual charm.
3. Just before serving, drizzle lightly with balsamic glaze if using.

This sweet and salty combo balances the fire and water elements—perfect for the Solstice! Watermelon holds the refreshing essence of Water, while feta brings Earth's richness. Mint adds a breeze of Air magic, and the entire dish radiates joy, love, and abundance—ideal for handfastings, feasts, or offerings under the sun.

Chilled Honeyed Cherry Fool

Ingredients
(Serves 4)

- 2 cups fresh cherries, pitted (plus a few extra for garnish)
- 2 tbsp honey (or maple syrup for vegan)
- 1 tsp lemon juice
- 1 cup heavy cream or coconut cream (chilled)
- ½ tsp vanilla extract

Method

1. In a small saucepan, combine cherries, honey, and lemon juice. Simmer gently over medium heat until cherries soften and begin to break down (about 10–12 minutes). Let cool completely.
2. Once cool, mash or blend into a chunky purée.
3. In a separate bowl, whip the cream with vanilla until soft peaks form.
4. Gently fold the cherry mixture into the cream, creating a marbled effect rather than fully mixing.
5. Spoon into individual glasses or bowls and chill for at least 1 hour before serving. Garnish with fresh cherries.

Cherries are little red symbols of passion, vitality, and joy—perfect for the peak of the sun's power. This dessert brings a balance of sweetness and lightness, and its swirling pink clouds feel like a solstice sunset in a cup.

Midsummer Berry Crumble Bars

Ingredients
(Makes 12 bars)

For the crust & crumble topping:
- 1½ cups rolled oats
- 1 cup plain flour (or almond flour for gluten-free)
- ½ cup brown sugar or coconut sugar
- ½ tsp cinnamon
- ¼ tsp salt
- ½ cup cold unsalted butter (or vegan butter), cut into cubes
- 1–2 tbsp cold water if needed

For the berry filling:
- 2 cups mixed berries (fresh or frozen – raspberries, strawberries, blueberries)
- 2 tbsp maple syrup or honey
- 1 tbsp cornflour or arrowroot powder
- 1 tsp lemon juice
- Optional: ½ tsp vanilla extract

Method

1. Preheat oven to 350°F (175°C). Line an 8x8-inch baking pan with parchment.
2. In a bowl, mix oats, flour, sugar, cinnamon, and salt. Cut in the butter using a fork or fingers until crumbly.
3. Press two-thirds of the mixture into the prepared pan to form a crust.
4. In another bowl, toss berries with syrup, lemon juice, cornflour, and vanilla if using. Spread over crust.
5. Sprinkle remaining crumble over the top.
6. Bake for 30–35 minutes until topping is golden and berries are bubbling.
7. Cool completely before cutting into bars.

These luscious berry bars are infused with Midsummer magic—ripe fruits of the land held together with golden oats and grains. Each bite celebrates the sweetness of life, the blessings of nature, and the joy of gathering under the sun. Perfect for picnics, spellwork, or a sunlit garden feast.

Lemon Balm & Lavender Sun Tea

Ingredients
(Makes about 1.5 litres / 6 cups)

- 3 sprigs fresh lemon balm (or 1 tbsp dried)
- 1 tsp dried lavender buds (culinary grade)
- 1 slice of lemon
- 1–2 tsp honey or agave syrup (optional)
- 6 cups fresh cold water
- A large glass jar with a lid

Method

1. Place the lemon balm, lavender, and lemon slice into a large glass jar or pitcher.
2. Fill with cold water and stir gently.
3. Cover and place in direct sunlight for 2–4 hours to infuse.
4. Strain out the herbs and lemon. Sweeten to taste with honey or agave.
5. Chill before serving, or pour over ice with a sprig of lemon balm for garnish.

This sun tea is steeped in solar energy—literally! Lemon balm uplifts the heart, while lavender calms the mind, making this an ideal potion for celebrating the balance of joy and peace at the summer solstice.

Litha Vanilla Rose Moon Milk

Ingredients
(Serves 2)

- 2 cups oat milk (or milk of choice)
- 1 tbsp rose water (culinary grade)
- 1 tsp vanilla extract
- 1–2 tsp honey or maple syrup (to taste)
- A tiny pinch of cinnamon or cardamom (optional)
- Edible rose petals for garnish (optional)

A dreamy moon milk for a dreamy night. Vanilla soothes, rose opens the heart, and oat milk brings a nurturing calm. Sip this under the twilight sky to gently welcome the moon as she rises on Litha's heels.

Method

1. In a small saucepan, warm the oat milk gently over low heat—don't let it boil.
2. Stir in the rose water, vanilla, and sweetener. Add a pinch of spice if using.
3. Whisk until steamy and well combined, then remove from heat.
4. Pour into mugs or teacups. Garnish with a sprinkle of dried rose petals if desired.

Peach & Thyme Solstice Spritz

Ingredients
(Serves 2–3)

- 1 ripe peach, sliced
- 2 sprigs fresh thyme (plus more for garnish)
- 1 tbsp honey or thyme simple syrup
- Juice of ½ lemon
- 1½ oz peach schnapps (optional for extra peachy punch)
- 4–6 oz dry white wine or prosecco
- Sparkling water or soda, to top
- Ice cubes

Method

1. In a shaker or jar, muddle the peach slices with honey and lemon juice. Add thyme sprigs and let sit for a couple of minutes.
2. Fill with ice, add schnapps (if using), and white wine or prosecco. Shake or stir gently.
3. Strain into glasses over fresh ice, top with sparkling water or soda to taste.
4. Garnish with a peach slice and a sprig of thyme.

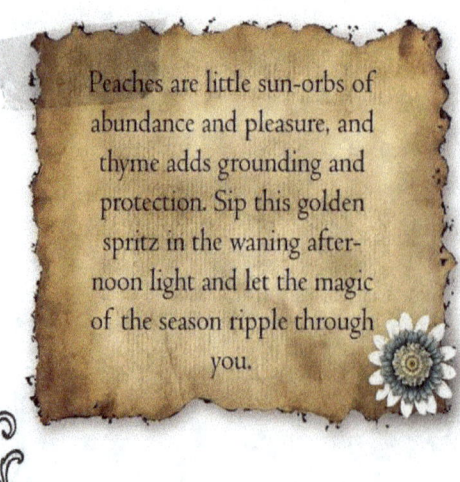

Peaches are little sun-orbs of abundance and pleasure, and thyme adds grounding and protection. Sip this golden spritz in the waning afternoon light and let the magic of the season ripple through you.

Sun-Kissed Berry Citrus Punch

Ingredients
(Serves 4–6)

- 1 cup strawberries, hulled and sliced
- 1 cup blueberries
- 1 orange, thinly sliced
- 1 lemon, thinly sliced
- 2 cups sparkling water or lemon-lime soda
- 1 cup orange juice (freshly squeezed if possible)
- ½ cup cranberry or pomegranate juice
- ¼ cup honey or agave syrup (optional for extra sweetness)
- A handful of fresh mint leaves
- Ice cubes

Optional (for a grown-up twist):
- ½ cup white wine or sparkling rosé

Method

1. In a large pitcher, combine sliced strawberries, blueberries, orange slices, lemon slices, and mint leaves.
2. Pour in orange juice and cranberry/pomegranate juice. Stir in honey or agave if desired.
3. Add sparkling water (or soda) just before serving for maximum fizz.
4. Fill glasses with ice and pour over the fruity mixture.
5. Garnish with extra mint and citrus slices for that extra pop of sunshine!

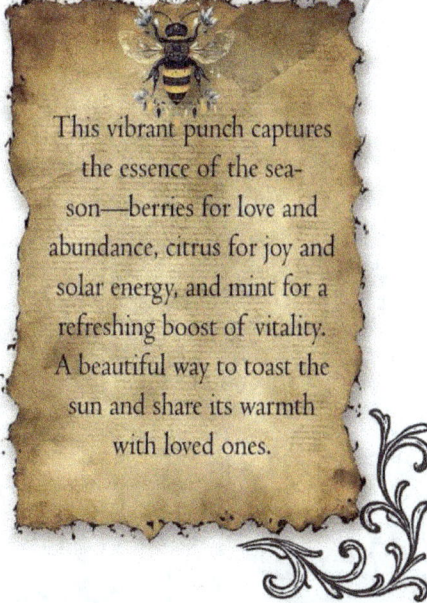

This vibrant punch captures the essence of the season—berries for love and abundance, citrus for joy and solar energy, and mint for a refreshing boost of vitality. A beautiful way to toast the sun and share its warmth with loved ones.

Quick-Pickled Cucumber & Radish
with Dill & Mustard Seeds

Ingredients
(Fills 1 large jar or 2 small ones)

- 1 cup thinly sliced cucumbers
- ½ cup thinly sliced radishes
- 1 cup water
- 1 cup white vinegar (or apple cider vinegar for a softer flavor)
- 1 tbsp sugar
- 1½ tsp salt
- 1 tsp mustard seeds
- ½ tsp black peppercorns
- 1 small garlic clove, crushed
- A few sprigs of fresh dill

Method

1. Pack sliced cucumber and radish into a clean jar with the garlic and dill.
2. In a saucepan, combine water, vinegar, sugar, salt, mustard seeds, and peppercorns. Bring to a boil, stirring to dissolve.
3. Pour the hot brine over the veggies until fully submerged.
4. Let cool, then seal and refrigerate. Best after 24 hours, keeps up to 2 weeks.

Pickling is a magical act of preservation—turning the fleeting freshness of early summer into something that lasts. Cucumber cools and cleanses, radish brings fire and courage, and dill protects. A crunchy little spell in every bite.

Strawberry-Rose Preserve

Ingredients
(Makes about 2 small jars)

- 500g fresh strawberries, hulled and halved
- 1½ cups sugar
- 1 tbsp fresh lemon juice
- 1 tsp rosewater (or to taste)
- Optional: 1 tsp dried culinary rose petals for texture and magic

Method

1. In a heavy saucepan, combine strawberries, sugar, and lemon juice. Let sit for 15–30 mins to macerate.
2. Bring to a gentle boil over medium heat, stirring often.
3. Cook for 20–30 minutes, skimming foam, until thickened (or until it passes the wrinkle test on a chilled plate).
4. Stir in rosewater and petals, then simmer for 1–2 more minutes.
5. Spoon into sterilized jars and seal. Keep refrigerated or water-bath can for longer storage.

Strawberries are sacred to Freyja, and rose is the flower of love and enchantment. This preserve captures the sweetness of Litha and seals it in a jar to be savored when the days grow shorter.

Thyme Simple Syrup

Ingredients
(Makes about 1 cup)

- 1 cup water
- 1 cup sugar
- 5–6 fresh thyme sprigs (or 2 tsp dried thyme)

Method

1. In a small saucepan, combine water and sugar. Heat gently, stirring until the sugar dissolves completely.
2. Add the thyme sprigs and simmer on low for 5 minutes.
3. Remove from heat, cover, and let steep for 15–20 minutes for full herbal flavor.
4. Strain out the thyme and pour syrup into a clean glass bottle or jar.
5. Store in the fridge for up to 2 weeks.

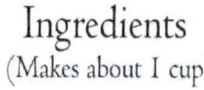

Thyme isn't just for potatoes! It brings clarity, courage, and protection to your spellwork and your sips. Use this syrup in cocktails, lemonades, iced teas—or even brushed on warm cake for a fragrant finish.

Ingredients

Method

Lammas: A Celebration of the First Harvest

As the golden fields sway under the late summer sun, the Wheel of the Year turns once more to Lammas — also known as Lughnasadh. This sacred festival, celebrated around August 1st, honors the first harvest and the life-giving gifts of the Earth. It is a time of both gratitude and gathering, of feasting and reflection, as we acknowledge the bounty that will sustain us through the coming darker months.

The word Lammas comes from the Old English hlaf-mas, meaning "loaf mass," a reference to the baking of the first breads from the season's new grain. Ancient traditions often centered around offering the first sheaves of wheat to the gods and goddesses of the land. In Celtic lore, this festival is closely tied to Lugh, the radiant god of skill and the harvest, whose energy blesses the fruits of our labor.

At Lammas, bread is sacred. Grains — wheat, barley, corn, oats — symbolize the sun's energy stored in physical form, transformed into nourishment by human hands. Sharing food at this time was (and still is) an act of magic, weaving bonds of community, gratitude, and hope for continued abundance. In this collection, you'll find recipes that honor the spirit of Lammas: hearty breads, sun-drenched vegetables, sweet fruits at their peak, and comforting preserves to savor the season's blessings. Every dish is a prayer of thanks — a joyful celebration of Earth's generosity and the work of our own hands. Whether you gather around a table with loved ones, walk barefoot through golden fields, or simply offer a loaf to the land in gratitude, may these recipes nourish your body and soul as you walk the sacred path of the harvest. Blessed Lammas!

Lammas Invocation

O radiant Sun, whose golden rays
Have ripened field and orchard's praise,
We honor now Thy sacred light,
That fills our hearths and hearts tonight.
Gracious Earth, so rich and deep,
Who cradles every seed we keep,
We thank Thee for Thy endless grace,
The fruits and grains, the sweet embrace.
Spirits of Harvest, Lords and Queens,
Who dance between the rows of green,
Bless these gifts our hands have made,
This feast from soil and sun and blade.
With every loaf, with every seed,
We honor work, we honor need.
With grateful hearts, we now partake,
The blessings of the life we make.
So by grain, and fruit, and honeyed wine,
We give our thanks, O Powers Divine.
Blessed be this Lammas Day,
As summer's light begins to wane.

☀ Lammas Blessing ☀

Bless the hands that plant the seed,
Bless the sun that grants the need,
Bless the rain that cools the land,
Bless the work of heart and hand.
From golden fields to kneading bowl,
From bursting vine to brimming soul,
May every meal, both small and grand,
Be seasoned with the Earth's own hand.
In every loaf and every stew,
May gratitude and joy shine through.
As harvest's bounty fills our days,
We walk the sunlit, sacred ways.
Blessed be this Lammas tide —
Abundance shared, and love beside.

Golden Sunflower Bread

Ingredients
(Makes 1 loaf)

- 2 cups bread flour
- 1 cup whole wheat flour
- 1 tbsp honey
- 1 tsp salt
- 1 packet active dry yeast
- 1 cup warm milk (110°F/43°C)
- ¼ cup sunflower seeds
- 2 tbsp olive oil
- 1 tbsp lemon juice
- 1 egg, beaten (for brushing)

Method

1. In a large bowl, mix the bread flour, whole wheat flour, salt, and yeast.
2. Combine the warm milk, honey, and olive oil, then slowly add it to the flour mixture, stirring until a dough forms.
3. Knead the dough for 8–10 minutes until it's smooth and elastic, adding flour if necessary.
4. Add the sunflower seeds and lemon juice, continuing to knead until evenly incorporated.
5. Let the dough rise in an oiled bowl for about 1 hour, or until doubled.
6. Preheat the oven to 375°F (190°C). Punch the dough down, shape it into a loaf, and place it in a greased loaf pan.
7. Brush the top of the dough with the beaten egg for a golden finish.
8. Bake for 25–30 minutes, or until the bread sounds hollow when tapped.
9. Cool on a wire rack before slicing.

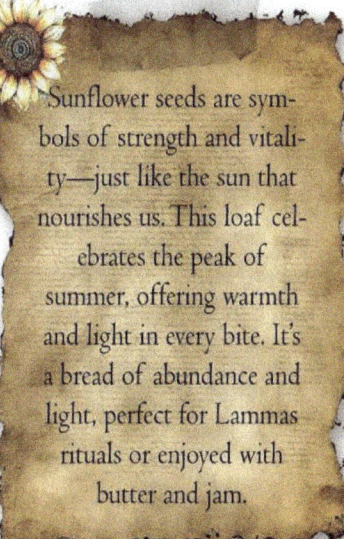

Sunflower seeds are symbols of strength and vitality—just like the sun that nourishes us. This loaf celebrates the peak of summer, offering warmth and light in every bite. It's a bread of abundance and light, perfect for Lammas rituals or enjoyed with butter and jam.

Lammas Seed Crackers

Ingredients
(Makes about 20 crackers)

- 1 cup all-purpose flour
- ½ cup whole wheat flour
- 1 tsp salt
- 1 tbsp olive oil
- 2 tbsp sunflower seeds
- 2 tbsp pumpkin seeds
- 1 tbsp sesame seeds
- ¼ cup cold water

Method

1. Preheat the oven to 375°F (190°C) and line a baking sheet with parchment paper.
2. In a large bowl, mix the flours and salt. Add the olive oil and seeds, stirring until combined.
3. Gradually add the cold water and knead until a smooth dough forms.
4. Roll out the dough on a lightly floured surface to about ¼-inch thickness.
5. Use a sharp knife or pizza cutter to cut the dough into squares or rectangles.
6. Place the crackers on the prepared baking sheet and bake for 12–15 minutes, or until golden and crisp.
7. Let cool completely before serving.

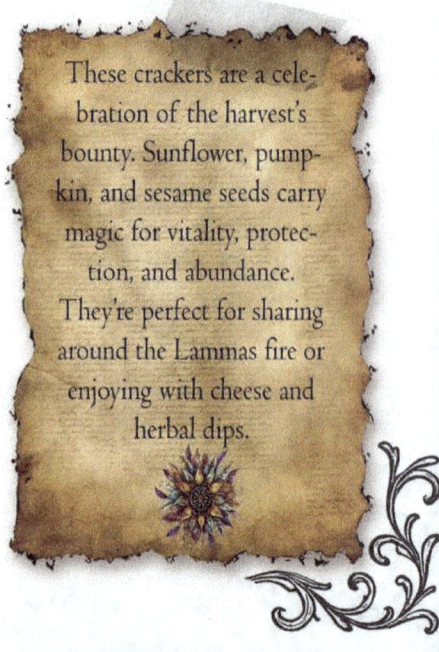

These crackers are a celebration of the harvest's bounty. Sunflower, pumpkin, and sesame seeds carry magic for vitality, protection, and abundance. They're perfect for sharing around the Lammas fire or enjoying with cheese and herbal dips.

Rustic Barley Bread

Ingredients
(Makes 1 loaf)

- 2 cups bread flour
- 1 cup barley flour
- 1 tbsp sugar
- 1 tsp salt
- 1 packet active dry yeast
- 1½ cups warm water
- 2 tbsp olive oil
- 1 tbsp honey

Method

1. In a large bowl, combine bread flour, barley flour, sugar, salt, and yeast.
2. In a separate bowl, mix warm water, olive oil, and honey. Slowly add to the dry ingredients, stirring to form a dough.
3. Knead the dough for 8–10 minutes until smooth, adding flour as needed.
4. Let the dough rise in a greased bowl for about 1 hour, or until doubled.
5. Preheat the oven to 375°F (190°C). Punch down the dough and shape it into a round loaf.
6. Place the loaf on a parchment-lined baking sheet, cover, and let rise for 30 minutes.
7. Bake for 30–35 minutes, or until golden and hollow-sounding when tapped.
8. Cool on a wire rack before slicing.

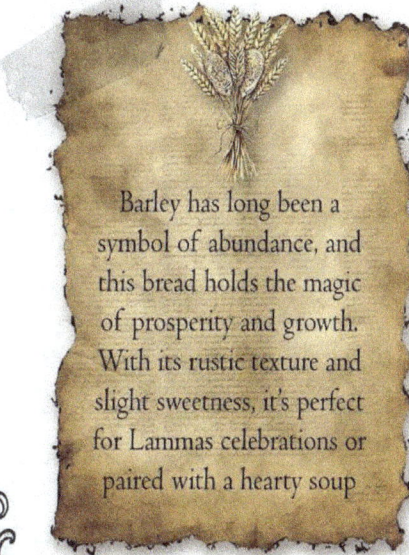

Barley has long been a symbol of abundance, and this bread holds the magic of prosperity and growth. With its rustic texture and slight sweetness, it's perfect for Lammas celebrations or paired with a hearty soup

Sun-dried Tomato & Basil Bread

Method

1. In a large bowl, combine the all-purpose and whole wheat flours, sugar, salt, and yeast.
2. In a separate bowl, mix the warm water, olive oil, and honey. Add to the dry ingredients, stirring to form a dough.
3. Knead for about 8–10 minutes, adding flour as needed, until the dough is smooth and elastic.
4. Add the sun-dried tomatoes, basil, oregano, and garlic powder, kneading them into the dough.
5. Place the dough in an oiled bowl, cover with a damp towel, and let rise for 1 hour or until doubled in size.
6. Preheat the oven to 375°F (190°C). Punch down the dough and shape it into a loaf. Place it on a baking sheet lined with parchment paper.
7. Let it rise for another 20–30 minutes, then bake for 30–35 minutes, or until golden brown.
8. Cool on a wire rack before slicing.

Ingredients
(Makes 1 loaf)

- 2 cups all-purpose flour
- 1 cup whole wheat flour
- 1 tbsp sugar
- 1 tsp salt
- 1 packet active dry yeast
- 1 cup warm water (110°F/43°C)
- 1 tbsp olive oil
- ½ cup chopped sun-dried tomatoes (packed in oil, drained)
- ¼ cup chopped fresh basil
- 1 tbsp dried oregano
- ½ tsp garlic powder
- 1 tbsp honey (for a touch of sweetness)

This aromatic bread brings the warmth of summer gardens into your home. Sun-dried tomatoes for vitality, basil for harmony, and garlic for protection—each bite is infused with the energies of Lammas harvest. Perfect for your feasts or as a gift of abundance!e.

Caramelized Onion & Goat Cheese Tartlets

Ingredients
(Makes 6 tartlets)

- 1 sheet puff pastry, thawed
- 2 large onions, thinly sliced
- 2 tbsp butter
- ½ cup crumbled goat cheese
- Fresh thyme leaves
- Salt & pepper to taste

Earthy and luxurious — these tartlets honor the sweet patience of the harvest.

Method

1. In a skillet, melt butter and cook onions slowly until caramelized, about 25–30 minutes.
2. Cut puff pastry into circles and press into tartlet pans or a muffin tin.
3. Fill with caramelized onions, sprinkle with goat cheese, thyme, salt, and pepper.
4. Bake at 190°C (375°F) for 20 minutes or until golden.

Cornbread with Fresh Herbs

Ingredients
(Makes 12 servings)

- 1 cup cornmeal
- 1 cup all-purpose flour
- 2 tbsp sugar
- 1 tbsp baking powder
- 1 tsp salt
- 1 tsp dried thyme
- 1 tbsp fresh rosemary, chopped
- 1 cup buttermilk
- 2 eggs
- ½ cup melted butter

Method

1. Preheat the oven to 375°F (190°C) and grease a 9-inch baking pan.
2. In a large bowl, mix the cornmeal, flour, sugar, baking powder, salt, thyme, and rosemary.
3. In a separate bowl, whisk together the buttermilk, eggs, and melted butter.
4. Add the wet ingredients to the dry ingredients and stir until just combined.
5. Pour the batter into the prepared pan and smooth the top.
6. Bake for 20–25 minutes, or until a toothpick inserted in the center comes out clean.
7. Let cool slightly before slicing and serving.

This cornbread carries the earthy energy of Lammas, with rosemary and thyme adding both flavor and magical properties. Rosemary for remembrance and protection, thyme for courage and purification. A perfect side for your harvest feast!

Fresh Tomato Tart

Ingredients
(Makes 1 tart)

- 1 sheet puff pastry (or pie dough)
- 4–5 medium tomatoes, thinly sliced
- 1 cup ricotta cheese
- ½ cup grated Parmesan cheese
- 2 tbsp fresh basil, chopped
- 1 tsp dried oregano
- Salt and pepper to taste
- Olive oil for drizzling

Method

1. Preheat the oven to 375°F (190°C) and line a baking sheet with parchment paper.
2. Roll out the puff pastry and place it on the prepared baking sheet.
3. Spread the ricotta cheese evenly over the pastry, leaving a small border around the edges.
4. Layer the tomato slices over the ricotta, slightly overlapping, until the entire surface is covered.
5. Sprinkle with Parmesan cheese, basil, oregano, salt, and pepper.
6. Drizzle with a little olive oil.
7. Bake for 25–30 minutes, or until the pastry is golden and crispy.
8. Allow to cool slightly before slicing and serving.

Tomatoes are symbols of the sun's warmth and vitality, and this tart celebrates the abundance of summer's ripest fruits. The creamy ricotta and fresh herbs bring a touch of freshness to your Lammas meal, while the sun-kissed tomatoes bring brightness and joy.

Garlic & Herb White Bean Dip

Ingredients
(Serves 6 as an appetizer)

- 1 can (400g) cannellini beans, drained
- 2 cloves garlic, minced
- 3 tbsp olive oil
- 2 tbsp lemon juice
- 1 tbsp chopped fresh rosemary or thyme
- Salt & pepper to taste

Method

1. Blend beans, garlic, olive oil, and lemon juice until smooth.
2. Stir in fresh herbs, salt, and pepper.
3. Serve with crackers, breads, or vegetable sticks.

Beans bring nourishing earth energy—perfect for grounding and community.

Grilled Eggplant
with Garlic & Mint

Ingredients
(Serves 4)

- 2 medium eggplants, sliced into rounds
- 2 tbsp olive oil
- 2 cloves garlic, minced
- 2 tbsp fresh mint, finely chopped
- Salt & pepper to taste
- Lemon wedges, to serve

Method

1. Brush eggplant slices with olive oil and season.
2. Grill over medium-high heat 2–3 minutes per side, until tender and charred.
3. Sprinkle with garlic and mint while warm.
4. Serve with lemon wedges.

: Eggplant absorbs the sun's fire—perfect for Lammas gratitude meals!

Herb-Marinated Chicken Skewers

Ingredients
(Serves 4)

- 500g (1 lb) chicken breast or thigh, cubed
- 3 tbsp olive oil
- 1 tbsp lemon juice
- 1 tbsp chopped rosemary
- 1 tbsp chopped thyme
- 1 tsp paprika
- Salt & pepper to taste
- Wooden skewers, soaked in water

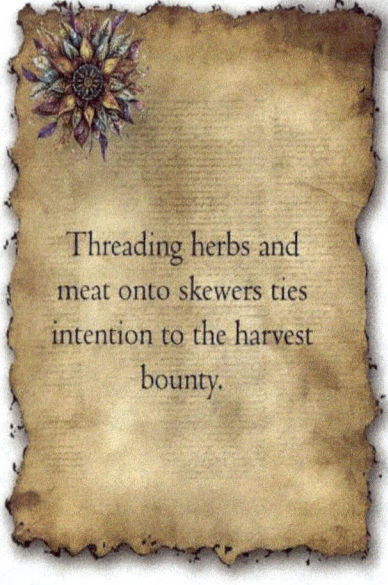

Threading herbs and meat onto skewers ties intention to the harvest bounty.

Method

1. Mix olive oil, lemon juice, herbs, paprika, salt, and pepper.
2. Toss chicken in marinade. Cover and refrigerate 1–2 hours.
3. Thread onto skewers and grill over medium heat until cooked through, about 10–12 minutes, turning occasionally.

Peach & Cream Cheese Pastries

Ingredients
(12 pastries)

- 1 sheet puff pastry, thawed
- 4 oz (120g) cream cheese, softened
- 2 tbsp honey
- 1 tsp vanilla extract
- 2 ripe peaches, thinly sliced
- 1 egg (for egg wash)

Method

1. Preheat oven to 200°C (400°F).
2. Mix cream cheese, honey, and vanilla until smooth.
3. Cut pastry into squares, spread cream cheese mixture in center, and top with peach slices.
4. Fold corners toward center, brush with egg wash, and bake 15–18 minutes.

Peaches bring prosperity; these little pastries capture summer's golden heart.

Roasted Vegetable Galette

Ingredients
(Makes 1 galette)

- 1 sheet puff pastry (or pie dough)
- 1 medium zucchini, sliced
- 1 medium yellow squash, sliced
- 1 red bell pepper, sliced
- 1 tbsp olive oil
- 1 tsp dried oregano
- 1 tsp garlic powder
- Salt and pepper to taste
- 1 egg, beaten (for brushing)
- 1 tbsp fresh basil, chopped (for garnish)

Method

1. Preheat the oven to 375°F (190°C) and line a baking sheet with parchment paper.
2. Toss the zucchini, yellow squash, and bell pepper with olive oil, oregano, garlic powder, salt, and pepper.
3. Arrange the vegetables in a single layer on a baking sheet and roast for 15 minutes, or until tender.
4. Roll out the puff pastry on a lightly floured surface and transfer it to the prepared baking sheet.
5. Pile the roasted vegetables in the center of the pastry, leaving a border around the edges.
6. Fold the edges of the pastry over the vegetables to form a rustic galette.
7. Brush the exposed pastry with the beaten egg.
8. Bake for 25–30 minutes, or until the pastry is golden and crisp.
9. Garnish with fresh basil before serving.

This galette embodies the abundance of summer's harvest, with vibrant vegetables bursting with the energy of the earth. It's a perfect dish to celebrate Lammas, filled with the magic of renewal and growth. The flaky pastry and roasted vegetables represent the balance between earth and sun.

Rosemary Roasted Potato Wedges

Ingredients
(Makes 4 servings)

- 4 large russet potatoes, cut into wedges
- 2 tbsp olive oil
- 2 tsp fresh rosemary, chopped
- 1 tsp garlic powder
- Salt and pepper to taste

Method

1. Preheat the oven to 400°F (200°C) and line a baking sheet with parchment paper.
2. Toss the potato wedges in olive oil, rosemary, garlic powder, salt, and pepper.
3. Spread the wedges in a single layer on the prepared baking sheet.
4. Roast for 35–40 minutes, flipping halfway through, until golden and crispy.
5. Let cool slightly before serving.

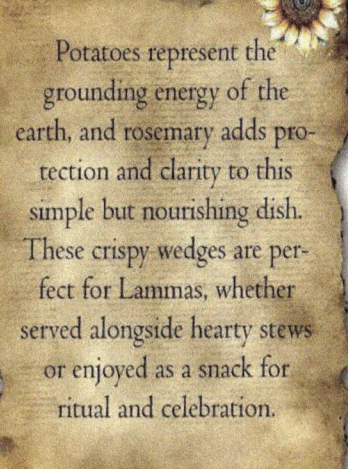

Potatoes represent the grounding energy of the earth, and rosemary adds protection and clarity to this simple but nourishing dish. These crispy wedges are perfect for Lammas, whether served alongside hearty stews or enjoyed as a snack for ritual and celebration.

Summer Squash Casserole

Ingredients
(Makes 6 servings)

- 3 medium yellow squash, sliced
- 2 tbsp olive oil
- 1 small onion, chopped
- 1 garlic clove, minced
- 1 cup shredded cheddar cheese
- 1 cup breadcrumbs
- 1 tsp dried thyme
- Salt and pepper to taste
- 1 egg, beaten

Method

1. Preheat the oven to 375°F (190°C) and grease a 9-inch casserole dish.
2. Heat olive oil in a large pan over medium heat. Add the onion and garlic, and sauté for 5 minutes until softened.
3. Add the sliced squash to the pan and cook for another 5–7 minutes until tender. Season with salt, pepper, and thyme.
4. In a bowl, combine the cooked squash mixture with the beaten egg, breadcrumbs, and half of the shredded cheese. Stir well.
5. Transfer the mixture to the prepared casserole dish and top with the remaining cheese.
6. Bake for 20–25 minutes, or until the top is golden and bubbly.
7. Let cool slightly before serving.

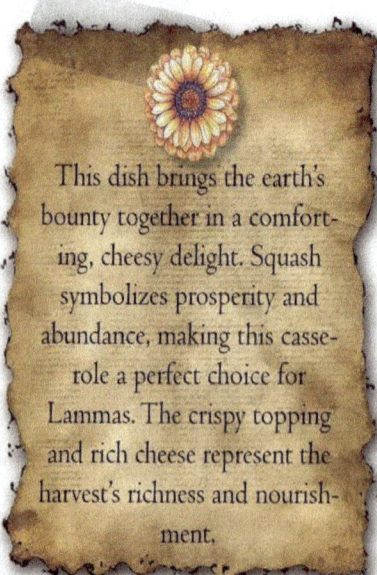

This dish brings the earth's bounty together in a comforting, cheesy delight. Squash symbolizes prosperity and abundance, making this casserole a perfect choice for Lammas. The crispy topping and rich cheese represent the harvest's richness and nourishment.

Sweet Corn & Honey Fritters

Ingredients
(Makes about 12 small fritters)

- 1 cup corn kernels (fresh or frozen)
- ¾ cup all-purpose flour
- 1 tbsp cornmeal
- 1 tsp baking powder
- ½ tsp salt
- 1 egg
- 1/3 cup milk
- 1 tbsp honey
- Oil for frying

Method

1. In a bowl, whisk flour, cornmeal, baking powder, and salt.
2. In another bowl, beat the egg with milk and honey.
3. Combine wet and dry ingredients, then stir in the corn kernels.
4. Heat oil in a skillet and drop spoonfuls of batter into the pan.
5. Fry until golden on each side, about 2–3 minutes per side.
6. Drain on paper towels and serve warm with extra honey if desired.

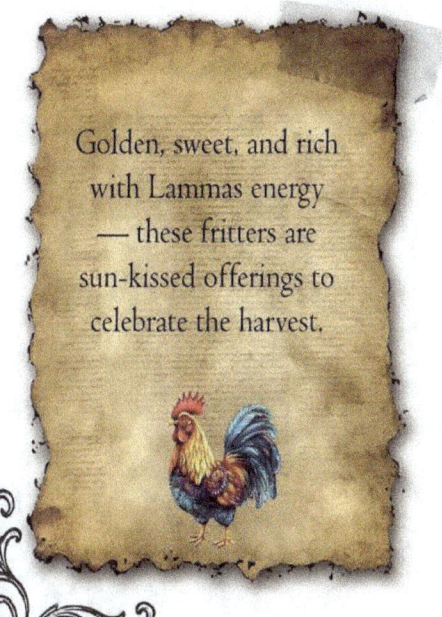

Golden, sweet, and rich with Lammas energy — these fritters are sun-kissed offerings to celebrate the harvest.

Zucchini & Sweet Corn Fritters

Ingredients
(Makes about 8 fritters)

- 1 cup grated zucchini
- ½ cup corn kernels
- ½ cup all-purpose flour
- ¼ cup grated Parmesan
- 1 egg
- 2 tbsp chopped green onions
- Salt & pepper to taste
- Oil for frying

Method

1. Squeeze excess moisture from the grated zucchini.
2. In a bowl, mix all ingredients until just combined.
3. Heat oil in a skillet and fry spoonfuls of batter until golden on both sides.
4. Drain on paper towels and serve hot.

These fritters weave the bounty of Lammas into every crispy, golden bite.

Golden Honeycomb Candy

Ingredients
(12 small cakes)

- 1 cup sugar
- ¼ cup honey
- ¼ cup water
- 1 tbsp baking soda

Method

1. Line a baking sheet with parchment paper.
2. Heat sugar, honey, and water in a heavy saucepan until golden (300°F/150°C).
3. Remove from heat and quickly whisk in baking soda—mixture will foam.
4. Pour immediately onto the sheet and let set. Break into shards once cool.

Bubbling golden honeycomb is pure solar magic—a sweet spell in every bite.

Honey & Almond Shortbread

Ingredients
(24 small cookies)

- 1 cup butter, softened
- ½ cup honey
- ½ cup powdered sugar
- 2¼ cups all-purpose flour
- ½ cup ground almonds
- ½ tsp salt
- 1 tsp vanilla extract

Method

1. Cream butter, honey, and sugar until light.
2. Add vanilla, then stir in flour, almonds, and salt.
3. Roll into small balls and flatten slightly on a baking sheet.
4. Bake at 175°C (350°F) for 10–12 minutes until edges are golden.

Honey and almonds are sacred to the harvest—bake these for offerings or simple summer joy.

Honey & Lavender Ice Cream

Ingredients
(Makes about 1 quart)

- 2 cups heavy cream
- 1 cup whole milk
- ½ cup honey
- 2 tbsp dried culinary lavender
- 5 egg yolks

Method

1. Heat cream, milk, and lavender until steaming. Steep 10 minutes, then strain.
2. Whisk egg yolks and honey together.
3. Slowly add warm cream to yolks, whisking.
4. Return mixture to the pot and cook gently until thickened.
5. Chill thoroughly, then churn in an ice cream maker.

Lavender soothes the spirit; honey calls abundance—this cooling treat blesses all senses at Lammas.

Lemon Balm Tea Cakes

Ingredients
(12 small cakes)

- 1 cup sugar
- ½ cup butter, softened
- 2 eggs
- 1½ cups all-purpose flour
- 1½ tsp baking powder
- ½ cup milk
- 2 tbsp finely chopped fresh lemon balm
- Zest of 1 lemon

Method

1. Cream butter and sugar. Add eggs one at a time.
2. Stir in flour, baking powder, lemon balm, zest, and milk.
3. Spoon into greased muffin tin.
4. Bake at 180°C (350°F) for 18–20 minutes.

Lemon balm brings calm and healing—perfect for a peaceful harvest gathering

Strawberry Lammas Bars

Ingredients
(16 squares)

- 1½ cups rolled oats
- 1 cup all-purpose flour
- ½ cup brown sugar
- ½ tsp cinnamon
- ¾ cup butter, melted
- 1½ cups strawberry jam

Method

1. Mix oats, flour, sugar, and cinnamon. Stir in melted butter.
2. Press 2/3 into a lined baking pan. Spread jam over, crumble remaining mixture on top.
3. Bake at 175°C (350°F) for 30–35 minutes until golden.

Strawberries are tied to love and luck—bake with a grateful heart for Lammas blessings.

Golden Honey Mead Spritzer

Ingredients
(Serves 4)

- 1½ cups traditional honey mead (or use a sweet white wine)
- 2 cups sparkling water or club soda
- 2 tbsp lemon juice
- Ice cubes
- Lemon slices and fresh mint for garnish

Mead, the drink of the gods, brings the spirit of ancient harvest feasts into modern celebrations.

Method

1. In a pitcher, combine mead, sparkling water, and lemon juice.
2. Stir gently.
3. Serve over ice, garnished with lemon slices and mint.

Herbal Lemonade for Lammas

Ingredients
(Serves 6)

- 6 cups cold water
- ¾ cup fresh lemon juice (about 4–5 lemons)
- ½ cup honey or sugar (adjust to taste)
- 2 tbsp fresh mint leaves
- 2 tbsp fresh basil leaves
- Lemon slices, for serving

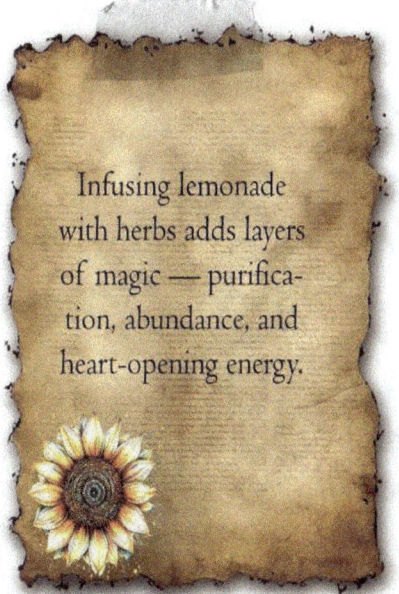

Infusing lemonade with herbs adds layers of magic — purification, abundance, and heart-opening energy.

Method

1. In a small saucepan, heat 1 cup water with honey/sugar until dissolved. Cool.
2. Muddle mint and basil leaves lightly.
3. In a large jug, combine lemon juice, syrup, herbs, and remaining water.
4. Chill and serve over ice with lemon slices.

Sweet Corn Silk Tea

Ingredients
(Makes about 4 cups)

- ¼ cup fresh or dried corn silk (organic, well-cleaned)
- 4 cups boiling water
- 1 tbsp honey (optional

Method

1. Place corn silk in a teapot.
2. Pour boiling water over and steep for 10–15 minutes.
3. Strain and sweeten if desired. Enjoy hot or iced.

An old folk remedy and blessing in a cup—corn silk tea connects you to the sacred cycle of growth and gratitude.

Blueberry & Lavender Jam

Ingredients
(Makes about 2 cups)

- 2 cups blueberries
- 1½ cups sugar
- 1 tbsp lemon juice
- 1 tsp dried culinary lavender buds

Method

1. In a saucepan, combine blueberries, sugar, and lemon juice.
2. Bring to a boil and simmer until thickened, about 20 minutes.
3. Stir in lavender during the last 5 minutes of cooking.
4. Pour into sterilized jars and seal.

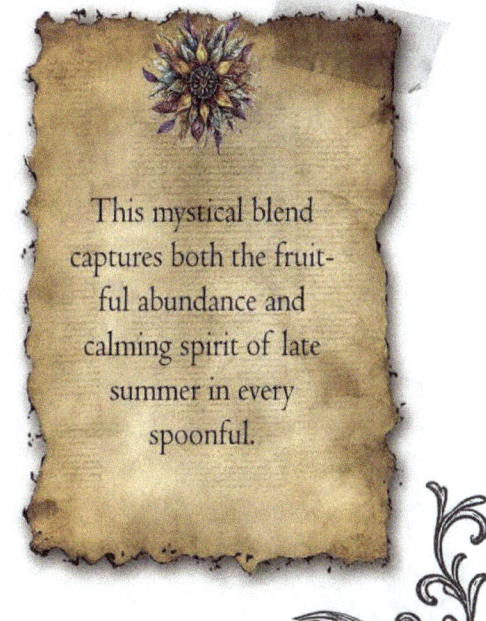

This mystical blend captures both the fruitful abundance and calming spirit of late summer in every spoonful.

Herbed Butter for Bread Blessing

Ingredients
(Makes ½ cup)

- ½ cup unsalted butter (softened)
- 1 tbsp fresh thyme, chopped
- 1 tbsp fresh rosemary, chopped
- 1 tsp fresh sage, chopped
- 1 tsp honey
- Pinch of salt

Method

1. In a small bowl, combine the softened butter, thyme, rosemary, sage, honey, and salt.
2. Mix until the herbs and honey are well incorporated into the butter.
3. Transfer the butter to a small serving dish, cover, and refrigerate until ready to serve.
4. Serve with freshly baked bread for a delicious Lammas feast.

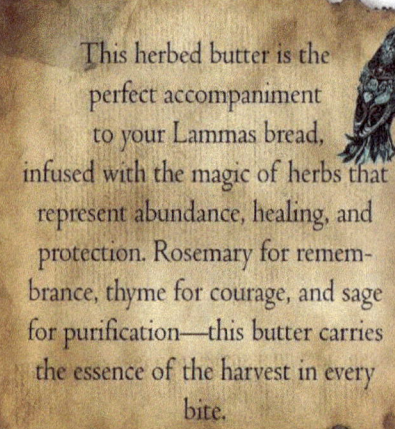

This herbed butter is the perfect accompaniment to your Lammas bread, infused with the magic of herbs that represent abundance, healing, and protection. Rosemary for remembrance, thyme for courage, and sage for purification—this butter carries the essence of the harvest in every bite.

Peach & Thyme Chutney

Ingredients
(Makes about 2 cups)

- 4 ripe peaches, peeled and diced
- ½ small red onion, finely chopped
- 1 tbsp grated fresh ginger
- 2 tbsp apple cider vinegar
- 2 tbsp brown sugar
- 1 tsp fresh thyme leaves
- ¼ tsp ground cinnamon
- Pinch of salt

Method

1. Combine all ingredients in a saucepan over medium heat.
2. Bring to a gentle simmer, stirring occasionally.
3. Cook for 20–25 minutes until thickened.
4. Cool and store in sterilized jars. Refrigerate and use within 2 weeks.

Preserving summer's sweetness, this chutney pairs beautifully with breads and cheeses for Lammas feasts.

Roasted Tomato & Garlic Relish

Ingredients
(Makes about 2 small jars)

- 2 cups cherry tomatoes, halved
- 4 cloves garlic, peeled
- 2 tbsp olive oil
- 1 tbsp balsamic vinegar
- 1 tsp sugar
- Salt & pepper to taste

Method

1. Toss tomatoes and garlic with olive oil, salt, and pepper.
2. Roast at 200°C (400°F) for 20–25 minutes until caramelized.
3. Blend or mash to your desired texture.
4. Stir in balsamic vinegar and sugar. Adjust seasoning.
5. Spoon into sterilized jars. Refrigerate and use within a week.

A vibrant, sun-drenched spread bursting with Lammas fire — a perfect companion for breads and cheeses.

Ingredients

Method

Welcome to the Feast of Mabon

As the wheel turns once more, we arrive at Mabon, the Autumn Equinox — a moment of perfect balance when day and night stand in harmony before the darker half of the year begins. Named after the Welsh god Mabon ap Modron, this sabbat honors the harvest and the deep gratitude we hold for the fruits of the earth. It is a time to gather, to reflect, and to prepare for the stillness to come.

Rooted in both ancient Celtic tradition and modern Pagan practice, Mabon marks the second of the three harvest festivals. While Lammas begins the reaping and Samhain closes it, Mabon celebrates the abundance at its peak. Grain has been threshed, fruit trees hang heavy, and the scent of ripe apples and bonfires drifts on the cooling breeze.

Food plays a sacred and central role in Mabon rites — not only as nourishment, but as offering and ritual. We bake to honor the grain spirits, roast to give thanks to the animals and plants that sustain us, and preserve the bounty to ensure abundance in the leaner months ahead. Whether shared at a table with loved ones or quietly savored in solitude, the meals of Mabon connect us to the earth, to each other, and to the rhythms that guide all life.

This collection of recipes celebrates the warmth, richness, and magic of Mabon — with ingredients that echo the season's gifts: apples, pumpkins, herbs, nuts, grains, and spices. Let each dish become a prayer of gratitude, a blessing for your hearth, and a remembrance of nature's sacred balance.

Blessed Mabon and merry feasting

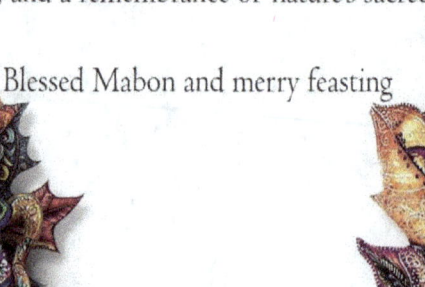

Mabon Invocation

As golden leaves drift to the earth,
We gather in balance, between light and dark.
At this turning of the Wheel,
We give thanks for the harvest, full and sweet.

Spirits of field, forest, and flame,
Bless this kitchen, this hearth, this home.
Infuse our hands with your wisdom,
Our food with your abundance.

Let apples be sacred,
Let grains be blessed,
Let every simmering pot
Be a prayer of gratitude.

We call upon the spirit of Mabon,
Child of the Mother, born of the Earth,
Guide us in harmony,
Teach us to release, to receive, to rest.

With every bite, we honor the land.
With every meal, we weave the magic of the season.
So mote it be.

Mabon Blessing

Bless this table, laid with care,
With autumn's gifts, so rich and rare.
Bless the hands that stirred and baked,
The hearts that gave, the love they make.

May all who gather, near or far,
Be warmed beneath the Harvest Star.
With grateful hearts and spirits bright,
We feast in balance, day and night.

As leaves fall soft and nights grow long,
May joy and peace be ever strong.
With every sip, with every bite,
We honour Earth and her delight.

Blessed be this Mabon meal.
So mote it be.

Cranberry Walnut Bread

Ingredients
(Makes 1 loaf)

- 2 cups flour
- 1 tsp baking soda
- ½ tsp salt
- ½ tsp cinnamon
- 1 cup chopped fresh or dried cranberries
- ½ cup chopped walnuts
- ¾ cup orange juice
- ½ cup honey or sugar
- 1 egg
- ¼ cup oil

Method

1. Preheat oven to 350°F (175°C). Grease a loaf tin.
2. In one bowl, whisk together flour, baking soda, salt, and cinnamon.
3. In another bowl, mix juice, sweetener, egg, and oil.
4. Combine wet and dry ingredients. Fold in cranberries and walnuts.
5. Pour into tin and bake for 45–55 minutes. Cool before slicing.

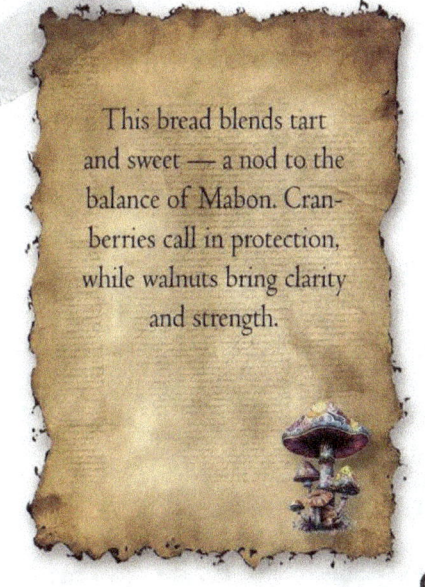

This bread blends tart and sweet — a nod to the balance of Mabon. Cranberries call in protection, while walnuts bring clarity and strength.

Cheddar & Chive Oat Biscuits

Ingredients
(Makes 12–14 biscuits)

- 1 cup rolled oats
- 1 cup all-purpose flour
- 1 tsp baking powder
- ½ tsp baking soda
- ½ tsp salt
- ½ cup cold butter, cubed
- 1 cup grated sharp cheddar
- 2 tbsp chopped fresh chives
- ½ cup buttermilk (plus extra for brushing)

These hearty oat biscuits are grounding and savory—perfect with soups, stews, or a cup of gratitude.

Method

1. Preheat oven to 400°F (200°C). Line a baking sheet.
2. Mix oats, flour, baking powder, soda, and salt.
3. Cut in butter until mixture resembles coarse crumbs.
4. Stir in cheese and chives, then mix in buttermilk until combined.
5. Drop spoonfuls onto tray or shape rounds.
6. Brush tops with extra buttermilk.
7. Bake 15–18 minutes until golden.

Fig & Hazelnut Honey Cake

Ingredients
(Serves 8–10)

- 1½ cups flour
- ½ cup ground hazelnuts
- ½ cup honey
- 1/3 cup sugar
- 2 eggs
- ½ cup milk
- ¼ cup butter, melted
- 1 tsp baking powder
- 1 tsp vanilla
- 5–6 fresh figs, sliced

Method

1. Preheat oven to 175°C (350°F). Grease a cake pan.
2. Mix dry ingredients in one bowl. In another, whisk eggs, honey, sugar, milk, butter, and vanilla.
3. Combine wet and dry ingredients, pour into pan, and top with figs.
4. Bake 30–35 minutes until golden and springy.

Figs and hazelnuts carry wisdom, protection, and a touch of Mabon luxury.

Pumpkin & Sage Scones

Ingredients
(Makes 8)

- 2 cups self-raising flour
- ¼ tsp salt
- ½ tsp ground cinnamon
- 6 tbsp cold butter, cubed
- ½ cup canned pumpkin
- ¼ cup milk (plus extra for brushing)
- 1 tbsp chopped fresh sage
- Optional: sprinkle of coarse sugar or sea salt

Method

1. Preheat oven to 400°F (200°C). Line a baking sheet.
2. In a large bowl, whisk flour, salt, and cinnamon.
3. Rub in the butter with fingertips until crumbly.
4. Stir in pumpkin, milk, and sage to form a soft dough.
5. Pat dough into a 1-inch thick round and cut into 8 wedges.
6. Place on tray, brush with milk, and sprinkle if desired.
7. Bake 15–20 minutes until golden.

Pumpkin brings protection and abundance, while sage offers wisdom and clearing—ideal energies to carry into autumn.

Spiced Apple & Walnut Muffins

Ingredients
(Makes 12 muffins)

- 2 cups all-purpose flour
- ½ cup brown sugar
- 2 tsp baking powder
- 1 tsp ground cinnamon
- ½ tsp ground nutmeg
- ½ tsp salt
- 2 eggs
- ½ cup melted butter
- ½ cup milk
- 1 tsp vanilla extract
- 1 ½ cups diced apples (peeled)
- ½ cup chopped walnuts

Apple and walnut carry energies of wisdom, grounding, and gratitude—perfect for Mabon reflection.

Method

1. Preheat oven to 375°F (190°C). Line or grease a 12-muffin tin.
2. In a large bowl, mix flour, sugar, baking powder, spices, and salt.
3. In another bowl, whisk eggs, melted butter, milk, and vanilla.
4. Combine wet and dry ingredients, then fold in apples and walnuts.
5. Fill muffin cups ¾ full and bake 20–25 minutes, or until a toothpick comes out clean.

Bacon-Wrapped Stuffed Chicken Breasts

Ingredients
(Serves 4)

- 4 chicken breasts
- 100g cream cheese
- 2 tbsp chopped fresh herbs (parsley, thyme, chives)
- ½ cup chopped spinach
- 8 rashers streaky bacon
- Salt & pepper

A dish of protection and nourishment — perfect for family gatherings and hearth blessings.

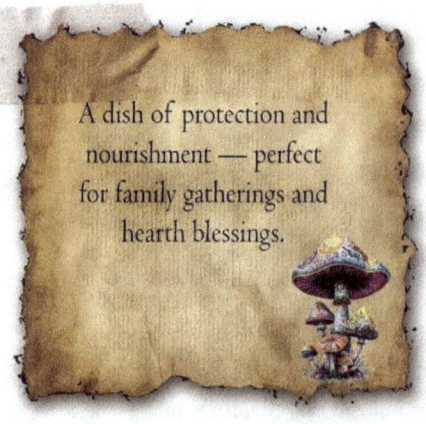

Method

1. Mix cream cheese, herbs, and spinach. Slice chicken to make pockets.
2. Fill each with cheese mixture. Wrap with bacon to seal.
3. Place in baking dish, bake at 200°C (390°F) for 30–35 mins until cooked through.

Beef & Ale Pie with Herby Crust

Ingredients
(Serves 6)

- 500g (1 lb) stewing beef, cubed
- 1 tbsp flour
- 1 tbsp olive oil
- 1 onion, chopped
- 1 carrot, chopped
- 1 cup mushrooms, sliced
- 1 cup dark ale or stout
- 1 cup beef stock
- 1 tsp thyme
- 1 sheet puff pastry or pie crust
- Salt & pepper

Method

1. Toss beef in flour, salt, and pepper. Brown in oil, remove.
2. Sauté onion, carrot, and mushrooms. Return beef. Add ale, stock, thyme.
3. Simmer 1.5 hrs until tender and thick. Cool slightly.
4. Transfer to pie dish. Top with pastry. Bake at 200°C (390°F) for 30–35 mins until golden.

Ale ties this dish to the land's grain harvest — beef adds grounding and strength as the days cool.

Mabon Harvest Galette

Ingredients
(Serves 6–8)

- 1 pie crust (homemade or store-bought)
- 2 apples, thinly sliced
- 1 pear, thinly sliced
- ¼ cup dried cranberries
- 2 tbsp brown sugar
- 1 tsp cinnamon
- 1 tsp lemon juice
- 1 tbsp butter, cubed
- 1 egg (for brushing)

Method

1. Preheat oven to 375°F (190°C). Line a baking sheet.
2. In a bowl, toss fruit, cranberries, sugar, cinnamon, and lemon juice.
3. Roll crust onto tray. Pile fruit mix in center, leaving 2 inches of edge.
4. Fold edges over fruit, pleating as needed. Dot with butter.
5. Brush crust with beaten egg.
6. Bake 35–40 minutes until golden and bubbling.

A rustic galette holds the spirit of the harvest—no fuss, full heart. Apples and pears bless us with health and sweetness.

Mabon Stuffed Acorn Squash

Ingredients
(Serves 4)

- 2 acorn squash, halved and seeded
- 1 tbsp olive oil
- 1 onion, chopped
- 2 garlic cloves, minced
- 1 apple, diced
- ½ cup chopped mushrooms
- 1 cup cooked wild rice or quinoa
- ¼ cup dried cranberries
- ¼ cup chopped pecans or walnuts
- 1 tsp rosemary
- Salt & pepper to taste

This dish symbolizes balance — sweet, savory, light, and hearty — a reflection of the equinox itself.

Method

1. Roast squash halves at 200°C (390°F) for 30–40 mins until tender.
2. Sauté onion, garlic, apple, and mushrooms in olive oil.
3. Add rice, cranberries, nuts, rosemary, salt, and pepper. Mix well.
4. Fill roasted squash with stuffing and bake 10 more mins.

Maple Pecan Baked Brie

Ingredients
(Serves 6–8 as an appetizer)

- 1 wheel of brie (8 oz)
- ¼ cup chopped pecans
- 2 tbsp maple syrup
- 1 sheet puff pastry, thawed
- 1 egg (for egg wash)
- Fresh rosemary (optional)

Method

1. Preheat oven to 400°F (200°C). Line a baking tray with parchment.
2. Place brie in center of puff pastry. Top with pecans and maple syrup.
3. Fold pastry over brie and seal. Brush with beaten egg.
4. Bake 20–25 minutes until golden. Let cool slightly before serving.
5. Garnish with rosemary if desired.

This rich dish balances heart and hearth—pecan for prosperity, brie for pleasure, and maple to sweeten the soul.

Mushroom & Chestnut Pot Pie

Ingredients
(Serves 4–6)

- 1 tbsp butter or oil
- 1 onion, chopped
- 2 garlic cloves, minced
- 2 cups mushrooms, sliced
- 1 cup cooked chestnuts, chopped
- 2 tbsp flour
- 1½ cups vegetable stock
- 1 tbsp tamari or soy sauce
- ½ tsp sage
- 1 sheet puff pastry or pie crust
- Salt & pepper to taste

Method

1. Sauté onion and garlic in butter/oil. Add mushrooms and cook until tender.
2. Stir in chestnuts, then flour. Cook 1 min.
3. Slowly add stock, tamari, sage, salt, and pepper. Simmer until thickened.
4. Pour into a baking dish. Cover with pastry and crimp edges.
5. Bake at 200°C (390°F) for 25–30 mins until golden.

Chestnuts and mushrooms carry grounding and protective energy — perfect for the introspective months ahead.

Pork & Apple Harvest Skillet

Ingredients
(Serves 4)

- 4 boneless pork chops
- 1 tbsp olive oil
- 1 apple, thinly sliced
- 1 red onion, sliced
- ½ cup apple cider or juice
- 1 tbsp wholegrain mustard
- 1 tsp fresh sage, chopped
- Salt & pepper to taste

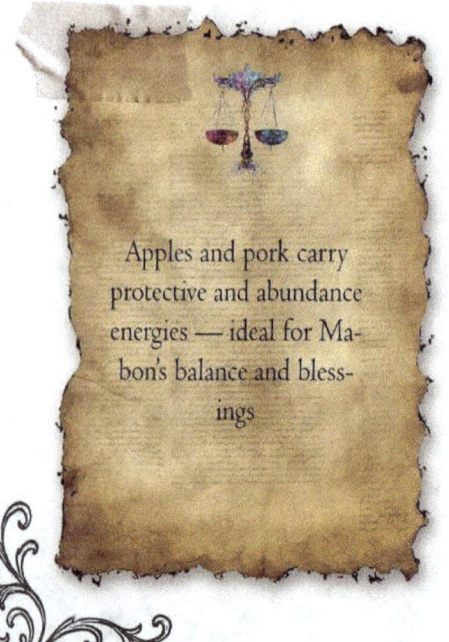

Apples and pork carry protective and abundance energies — ideal for Mabon's balance and blessings

Method

1. Heat oil in a skillet. Season and sear pork chops 3–4 mins each side. Remove and set aside.
2. In same pan, sauté onion and apple until soft.
3. Add cider, mustard, and sage. Simmer to reduce slightly.
4. Return pork to the pan and simmer 5 mins more.

Pumpkin & Sage Hand Pies

Ingredients
(Makes 6–8)
- 1 cup mashed pumpkin (fresh or canned)
- ½ tsp salt
- ½ tsp nutmeg
- 1 tsp fresh chopped sage
- ½ cup shredded cheese (cheddar or feta work well)
- Ready-made pie crust or puff pastry
- 1 egg (for egg wash)

Method

1. Preheat oven to 375°F (190°C). Line a baking tray with parchment paper.
2. In a bowl, mix pumpkin, salt, nutmeg, sage, and cheese.
3. Roll out pastry and cut into circles or rectangles.
4. Spoon filling onto half of each piece, fold, and seal edges with a fork.
5. Brush with egg wash and bake for 20–25 minutes until golden brown.

Pumpkin is a symbol of abundance and home magic. Paired with sage, it offers grounding, wisdom, and warmth for the turning season.

Blackberry & Apple Crumble

Ingredients
(Serves 6)

- 2 cups chopped apples
- 2 cups fresh or frozen blackberries
- ¼ cup brown sugar
- 1 tsp cinnamon
- 1 tbsp lemon juice

For the crumble topping:
- ½ cup rolled oats
- ½ cup flour
- 1/3 cup brown sugar
- ¼ cup butter, cold and cubed

Method

1. Preheat oven to 180°C (350°F).
2. Combine fruit, lemon juice, sugar, and cinnamon. Transfer to baking dish.
3. In a bowl, rub butter into oats, flour, and sugar until crumbly.
4. Sprinkle topping over fruit and bake for 30–35 minutes until golden.

This rustic crumble celebrates the wild harvest — abundance, protection, and joyful messes.

Roasted Root Veggie Medley

Ingredients
(Serves 4–6)

- 2 carrots, sliced
- 2 parsnips, sliced
- 1 beetroot, peeled and diced
- 1 small sweet potato, diced
- 2 tbsp olive oil
- 1 tsp dried rosemary
- ½ tsp salt
- ¼ tsp black pepper

Method

1. Preheat oven to 400°F (200°C).
2. Toss all vegetables with oil, rosemary, salt, and pepper.
3. Spread on a baking tray in a single layer.
4. Roast for 30–40 minutes, flipping halfway, until golden and tender.

Root vegetables pull energy from deep within the earth. Perfect for grounding your spirit as the days grow cooler and darker.

Caramel Apple Hand Pies

Ingredients
(Makes 6–8)

- 1 batch pie dough or 2 store-bought rounds
- 2 apples, diced
- ¼ cup caramel sauce
- 2 tbsp brown sugar
- 1 tsp cinnamon
- 1 egg (for brushing

Carry your harvest magic in your hand — apple for love, caramel for sweetness, and cinnamon for energy.

Method

1. Preheat oven to 190°C (375°F).
2. Mix apples with sugar, cinnamon, and caramel.
3. Roll out dough and cut into circles or squares.
4. Spoon filling onto half of each shape. Fold, seal edges with fork, and cut a steam slit.
5. Brush with beaten egg and bake for 20–25 minutes.

Chai-Spiced Rice Pudding

Ingredients
(Serves 4)

- ½ cup arborio or short-grain rice
- 2 cups milk (or plant-based)
- ¼ cup cream or coconut milk
- 3 tbsp brown sugar
- 1 tsp vanilla extract
- 1 tsp ground chai spice (or cinnamon, cardamom, and cloves)
- Optional: chopped pistachios or dried fruit for topping

Spiced and creamy, this pudding is soul-soothing comfort — a true hearth spell in a bowl.

Method

1. In a saucepan, combine rice, milk, and cream. Simmer on low, stirring often, for 25–30 minutes.
2. Add sugar, vanilla, and spices. Cook another 5 minutes until thickened.
3. Serve warm or chilled, topped with nuts or dried fruit.

Pear & Thyme Crumble

Ingredients
(Serves 4–6)

- 4 ripe pears, sliced
- 1 tbsp fresh lemon juice
- 1 tsp fresh thyme leaves
- 2 tbsp honey or brown sugar

For the topping:

- ½ cup oats
- ½ cup flour
- 1/3 cup brown sugar
- ¼ cup butter, chilled and cubed
- Pinch of salt

Method

1. Preheat oven to 375°F (190°C).
2. Toss pears with lemon juice, thyme, and sweetener. Place in baking dish.
3. In a bowl, mix topping ingredients and rub together to make crumbs.
4. Sprinkle topping over fruit. Bake for 30–35 minutes until golden and bubbly.

Pear is the fruit of love and wisdom. Paired with thyme's courage and clarity, this dessert celebrates the gentler gifts of the season.

Spiced Pear & Honey Tart

Ingredients
(Serves 8)

- 1 sheet puff pastry, thawed
- 3 ripe pears, thinly sliced
- 2 tbsp lemon juice
- ¼ cup honey (plus extra for drizzling)
- 1 tsp ground cinnamon
- ½ tsp ground nutmeg
- 1 tbsp butter, melted
- Optional: chopped walnuts for topping

Method

1. Preheat oven to 200°C (400°F).
2. Toss pear slices in lemon juice, cinnamon, nutmeg, and honey.
3. Lay puff pastry on a lined baking tray and fold the edges to form a border.
4. Arrange pears inside the border. Brush pears with melted butter.
5. Bake 20–25 minutes until golden.
6. Drizzle with honey and sprinkle with walnuts before serving.

Pears bring harmony and sweetness, perfect for grounding your spirit at harvest's end.

Chai-Spiced Hot Chocolate

Ingredients
(Serves 2)

- 2 cups milk of choice
- 2 tbsp cocoa powder
- 2 tbsp dark chocolate chips
- ¼ tsp cinnamon
- Pinch each: cardamom, ginger, cloves, black pepper
- 1 tsp vanilla
- Sweetener to taste

A decadent brew with the soul of Mabon — comfort, spice, and a reminder to rest..

Method

1. Heat all ingredients in a saucepan over low heat until melted and steamy.
2. Whisk until frothy and serve hot.

Elderberry & Hibiscus Fizz

Ingredients
(Serves 4)

- 1 cup dried hibiscus tea, steeped and cooled
- ½ cup elderberry syrup
- 1 tbsp lemon juice
- Sparkling water
- Ice

Method

1. Combine hibiscus tea, elderberry syrup, and lemon juice in a jug.
2. Fill glasses with ice and pour mixture halfway.
3. Top with sparkling water and gently stir.

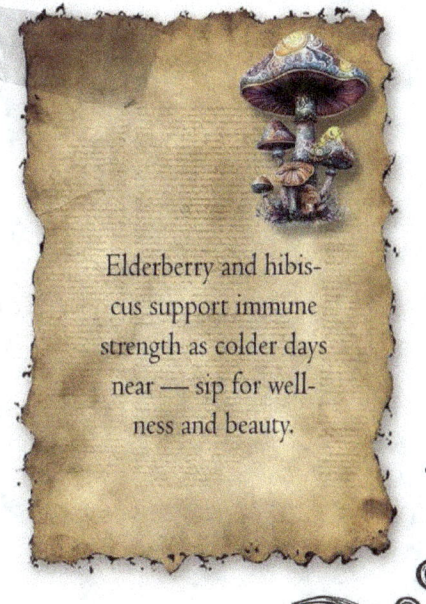

Elderberry and hibiscus support immune strength as colder days near — sip for wellness and beauty.

Mulled Blackberry & Apple Cider

Ingredients
(Serves 4–6)

- 4 cups apple cider
- 1 cup blackberry juice (or mash and strain fresh blackberries)
- 1 cinnamon stick
- 4 whole cloves
- 2 star anise
- 1 orange, sliced
- Honey or maple syrup to taste

Method

1. Combine all ingredients in a saucepan.
2. Simmer gently for 15–20 minutes without boiling.
3. Strain and serve warm, garnished with a slice of orange or star anise.

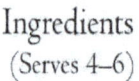

Blackberries honour the waning light, while apple invokes abundance — a warming drink for introspection and gratitude.

Rosemary Pear Sparkler

Ingredients
(Serves 4)

- 2 ripe pears, peeled and pureed
- 1 tbsp lemon juice
- 1 tsp honey or maple syrup
- Sparkling water or soda water
- 2 sprigs fresh rosemary
- Ice

Method

1. Muddle rosemary in a shaker with lemon juice and honey.
2. Add pear puree and shake with ice.
3. Strain into glasses and top with sparkling water.
4. Garnish with rosemary sprig or pear slice.

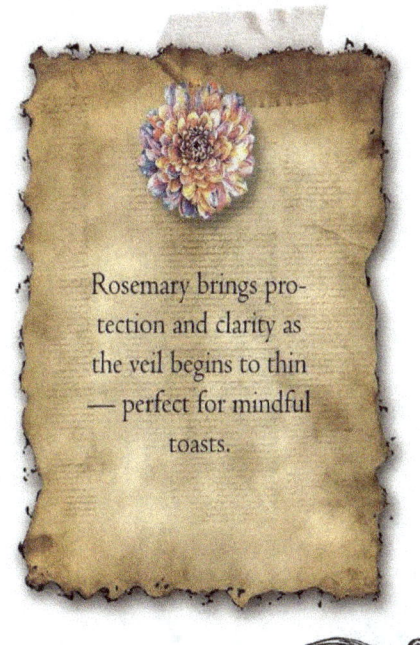

Rosemary brings protection and clarity as the veil begins to thin — perfect for mindful toasts.

Spiced Apple Cider

Ingredients
(Serves 6)

- 6 cups apple cider or unsweetened apple juice
- 1 orange, sliced
- 4 cinnamon sticks
- 6 whole cloves
- 4 allspice berries
- 1-inch piece fresh ginger, sliced
- Optional: 2 tbsp maple syrup or honey

Method

1. In a large pot, combine all ingredients.
2. Bring to a simmer over medium heat.
3. Reduce heat to low and simmer uncovered for 20–30 minutes.
4. Strain and serve warm, garnished with a cinnamon stick or orange slice.

Apple cider stirs up the energies of gratitude and protection. Sip this warming brew to honour the balance of light and dark.

Spiced Pumpkin Smoothie

Ingredients
(Serves 2)

- 1 cup pumpkin puree
- 1 frozen banana
- 1 cup oat or almond milk
- ½ tsp cinnamon
- ¼ tsp nutmeg
- 1 tbsp maple syrup
- 1 tsp vanilla extract

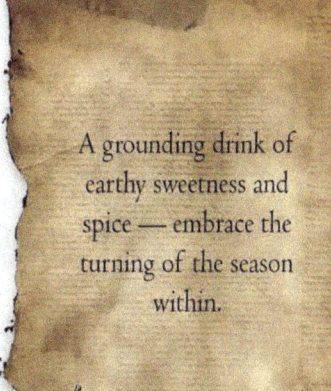

A grounding drink of earthy sweetness and spice — embrace the turning of the season within.

Method

1. Blend all ingredients until smooth.
2. Serve chilled with a sprinkle of cinnamon on top.

Mabon Berry & Lavender Jam

Ingredients
(Makes ~2½ cups)

- 2 cups mixed berries (blackberries, raspberries, blueberries)
- 1½ cups sugar
- 1 tbsp lemon juice
- 1 tsp dried culinary lavender

Method

1. In a saucepan, combine berries, sugar, and lemon juice.
2. Stir in lavender and bring to a gentle boil.
3. Simmer until thick (20–30 minutes), mashing berries as desired.
4. Jar and seal while hot.

Lavender soothes the heart while berries hold the last kiss of summer sun.

Pear & Ginger Jam

Ingredients
(Makes ~3 cups)

- 4 ripe pears, peeled and chopped
- 1 tbsp grated fresh ginger
- 1 tbsp lemon juice
- 1½ cups sugar
- ½ cup water

Method

1. Combine all ingredients in a saucepan.
2. Simmer on low, stirring often, until thickened (30–45 mins).
3. Blend or leave chunky.
4. Pour into sterilised jars and seal.

Pear and ginger spark both sweetness and fire — a balance of soft and sharp energies.

Pickled Red Onions with Thyme

Ingredients
(Makes 1 pint)

- 2 medium red onions, thinly sliced
- 1 cup apple cider vinegar
- 1 cup water
- 2 tbsp sugar
- 1½ tsp salt
- A few sprigs fresh thyme

Thyme offers courage and memory — this preserve sharpens mind and meal alike.

Method

1. Pack onions and thyme into a clean jar.
2. In a saucepan, heat vinegar, water, sugar, and salt until dissolved.
3. Pour hot brine over onions.
4. Cool, seal, and refrigerate. Ready in 1–2 days.

Pumpkin Chutney

Ingredients
(Makes ~2 cups)

- 2 cups peeled, diced pumpkin
- 1 apple, diced
- ½ onion, chopped
- ½ cup brown sugar
- ½ cup apple cider vinegar
- 1 tsp grated ginger
- ½ tsp cinnamon
- ¼ tsp chili flakes (optional)
- Pinch of salt

A spicy-sweet preserve of transformation — turning harvest into golden ritual.

Method

1. Combine all ingredients in a pot and bring to a boil.
2. Simmer uncovered for 40–50 minutes, stirring often, until thick.
3. Pour into sterilised jars and seal.

Spiced Apple Butter

Ingredients
(Makes ~2 cups)

- 6 medium apples, peeled, cored, and chopped
- ¾ cup brown sugar
- 1 tsp cinnamon
- ½ tsp nutmeg
- ¼ tsp cloves
- Pinch of salt
- 1 tsp vanilla extract

Method

1. Cook apples in a slow cooker or saucepan on low heat until soft (4–6 hours), stirring occasionally.
2. Mash or blend until smooth.
3. Add sugar and spices, then simmer uncovered until thick and spreadable.
4. Stir in vanilla and jar while hot.

Apple butter sweetens long nights — a preserve of comfort and hearth magic.

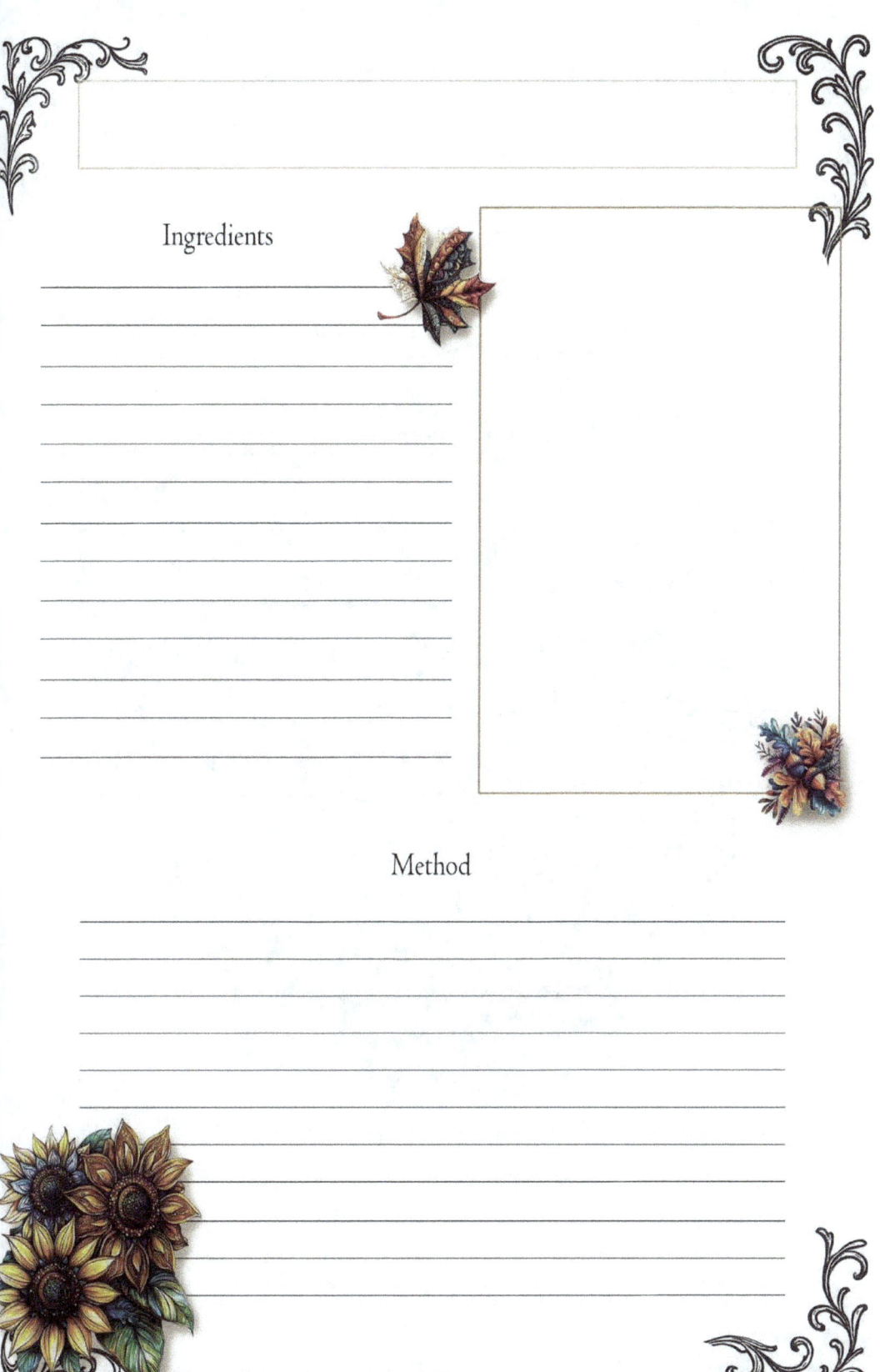

Ingredients

Method

Samhain: A Feast Beyond the Veil

Samhain (pronounced sow-in) marks one of the most sacred points on the Wheel of the Year — the witch's new year and a powerful festival of endings, beginnings, and remembrance. Traditionally celebrated from October 31st to November 1st in the Northern Hemisphere (and around April 30th to May 1st in the Southern Hemisphere), Samhain signals the final harvest, the darkening of the year, and the time when the veil between worlds is at its thinnest.

Rooted in ancient Celtic tradition, Samhain was the dividing line between summer's light and winter's darkness. Fires were lit, animals were culled, and offerings were made to honour ancestors and appease wandering spirits. It is a night of divination, shadow work, and deep spiritual reflection — but also of comfort, gathering, and shared warmth.

Food lies at the very heart of Samhain, carrying both symbolic weight and practical comfort. Traditional dishes often include final harvest fruits, roots, nuts, grains, and preserved goods. Breads and cakes were baked as offerings for the dead, while stews and hearty fare nourished the living against the coming cold. Sweet treats honour beloved spirits and children alike, echoing the ancient practice of leaving food at thresholds to welcome or ward off the unseen.

In this Samhain recipe collection, each dish is a ritual of its own — a spell woven from earth's last bounty, a remembrance of kin, a celebration of cyclical change. Whether you're baking soul cakes, simmering cider, or wrapping gifts for ancestral altars, may these recipes nourish your body, spirit, and sacred connection to the turning year.

Samhain Invocation

As the veil grows thin and shadows fall,
We gather at twilight to honour the call.
Spirits of old, come walk beside —
With love and light, the doors swing wide.

From hearth to altar, from spoon to flame,
We cook, we craft, we speak your name.
With herbs and spice, with fire and bread,
We weave the living with the dead.

By root and fruit, by bone and stone,
We bless this feast, this sacred home.
With every stir and every bite,
We kindle warmth through longest night.

Welcome, ancestors, kind and wise —
Share in our laughter, tears, and ties.
May this Samhain's gentle power
Guide us true through winter's hour.

Samhain Blessing

May the golden sun warm your spirit,
May the ripe earth fill your hands.
May your table be rich with the season's gifts,
And your heart be full of laughter and light.
May flowers bloom along your path,
And herbs whisper secrets in the breeze.
May joy rise like midsummer fire,
And love shine like the longest day.
Blessed be this Solstice hour—
A turning point, a celebration,
A feast for the soul and the senses.
Blessed Litha

Blood Orange & Clove Muffins

Ingredients
(Makes 12)

- 2 cups self-raising flour
- ½ cup brown sugar
- 1 tsp ground cloves
- ¼ tsp salt
- 2 eggs
- ½ cup milk
- ¼ cup melted butter
- 1/3 cup blood orange juice
- Zest of 1 blood orange

Method

1. Preheat oven to 180°C / 350°F. Line a muffin tin.
2. In a bowl, mix flour, sugar, cloves, and salt.
3. In another bowl, whisk eggs, milk, butter, juice, and zest.
4. Stir wet into dry until just combined.
5. Spoon into cases and bake 18–22 minutes.

Blood orange energizes the sacral and heart chakras, while clove offers protection. Perfect for rituals or quiet reflection.

Cider-Glazed Apple Bread

Ingredients
(Makes 1 loaf)
- 2 cups plain flour
- 1½ tsp baking powder
- ½ tsp salt
- ½ tsp cinnamon
- 2 eggs
- ½ cup sugar
- ½ cup apple cider
- ¼ cup vegetable oil
- 1 tsp vanilla
- 1½ cups peeled, diced apples

For the glaze:
- ¼ cup apple cider
- ½ cup icing sugar

Apples carry the energy of the Otherworld and the divine feminine. This sweet bread bridges the worlds with every bite.

Method
1. Preheat oven to 175°C / 350°F. Grease a loaf pan.
2. In a large bowl, combine flour, baking powder, salt, and cinnamon.
3. In another bowl, whisk eggs, sugar, cider, oil, and vanilla.
4. Mix wet into dry, then fold in apples.
5. Pour into the pan and bake 45–55 minutes.
6. Mix glaze ingredients. Drizzle over warm bread.

Cinnamon Hazelnut Braid

Ingredients
(Makes 1 loaf)

- 2¾ cups plain flour
- 2¼ tsp active dry yeast (1 packet)
- ¼ cup sugar
- ½ tsp salt
- ½ cup warm milk
- ¼ cup unsalted butter, melted
- 1 egg

For the filling:
- ¼ cup softened butter
- 1/3 cup brown sugar
- 2 tsp ground cinnamon
- ½ cup finely chopped toasted hazelnuts

Method

1. In a large bowl, combine 1 cup flour, yeast, sugar, and salt.
2. Add warm milk, melted butter, and egg. Mix well.
3. Gradually add remaining flour to form a soft dough. Knead for 6–8 minutes.
4. Place in an oiled bowl, cover, and let rise until doubled (about 1 hour).
5. Roll dough into a rectangle (about 10x14 inches). Spread with butter, then sprinkle with cinnamon, sugar, and nuts.
6. Roll up tightly from the long edge. Slice down the middle lengthwise, leaving one end attached.
7. Twist the two strands together, then form into a ring or coil.
8. Place on a lined tray, cover, and let rise 30–40 minutes.
9. Bake at 180°C / 350°F for 25–30 minutes, until golden. Cool before slicing.

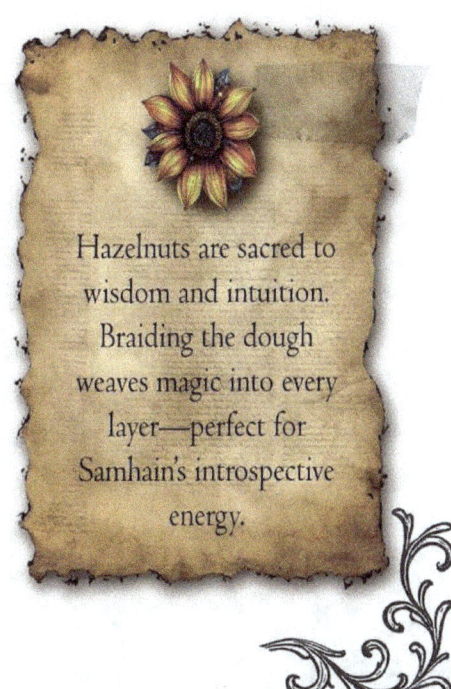

Hazelnuts are sacred to wisdom and intuition. Braiding the dough weaves magic into every layer—perfect for Samhain's introspective energy.

Midnight Ash Cake

Ingredients
(Serves 8–10)
- 1¾ cups plain flour
- ½ cup black cocoa powder (or regular cocoa + 1 tbsp activated charcoal)
- 1½ tsp baking powder
- ½ tsp salt
- 1 cup caster sugar
- 2 eggs
- ½ cup vegetable oil
- 1 cup buttermilk
- 1 tsp vanilla extract
- Optional: ½ tsp cinnamon or cardamom for warmth

For the glaze:
- ¾ cup icing sugar
- 2–3 tbsp strong brewed coffee or cold brew
- Pinch of charcoal or black food colouring (optional)

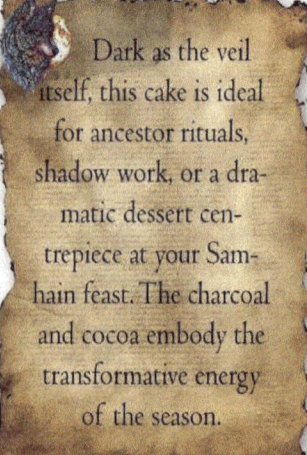

Dark as the veil itself, this cake is ideal for ancestor rituals, shadow work, or a dramatic dessert centrepiece at your Samhain feast. The charcoal and cocoa embody the transformative energy of the season.

Method

1. Preheat oven to 175°C (350°F). Grease and line a round or loaf cake tin.
2. In a bowl, sift flour, cocoa, baking powder, and salt.
3. In a separate bowl, whisk sugar, eggs, oil, buttermilk, and vanilla until smooth.
4. Gradually fold in the dry ingredients. Mix until just combined.
5. Pour into prepared tin and bake for 35–40 minutes or until a skewer comes out clean.
6. Cool before glazing.
7. For the glaze, mix icing sugar and coffee until pourable. Drizzle over cooled cake.

Shadow Moon Cookies

Ingredients
(Makes 24)

- 2 cups plain flour
- 1 cup unsalted butter, softened
- ½ cup icing sugar
- 1½ tsp vanilla extract
- 2 cups plain flour
- ½ cup finely ground almonds
- Extra icing sugar, for dusting
- Edible black food dust or cocoa, for shadowing

Method

1. Preheat oven to 160°C / 325°F. Line a tray with parchment.
2. Cream butter and sugar. Add vanilla, then flour and almonds.
3. Shape into crescent moons. Place on tray.
4. Bake 14–16 minutes until pale golden.
5. Cool slightly, then dust with icing sugar.
6. Use cocoa or food dust to shade one side like a shadowed moon.

Moon shapes honour the goddess and the cycles. These cookies reflect the balance of light and shadow at Samhain.

Spiced Soul Cakes for Samhain

Ingredients
(Makes 12 small cakes)

- 2 cups plain flour
- ½ tsp baking powder
- ½ tsp salt
- ½ tsp cinnamon
- ½ tsp nutmeg
- ¼ tsp ground cloves
- ½ cup unsalted butter, softened
- ¾ cup sugar
- 2 egg yolks
- ½ cup currants or raisins
- 2 tbsp milk

Method

1. Preheat oven to 180°C / 350°F. Line a baking sheet with parchment paper.
2. In a bowl, sift together flour, baking powder, salt, and spices.
3. In another bowl, cream butter and sugar until light. Beat in egg yolks.
4. Stir in the dry ingredients, then currants and milk. Mix to form a soft dough.
5. Roll out on a floured surface to ½-inch thick. Cut into rounds.
6. Place on the tray and score a cross on each.
7. Bake 12–15 minutes, until golden. Cool on a rack.

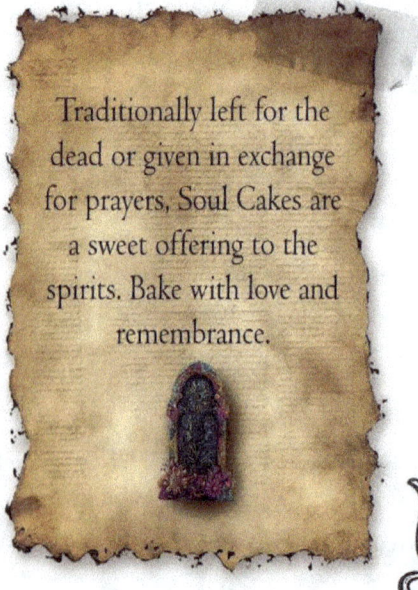

Traditionally left for the dead or given in exchange for prayers, Soul Cakes are a sweet offering to the spirits. Bake with love and remembrance.

Black Garlic & Mushroom Pie

Ingredients
(Serves 4–6)

- 2 tbsp butter or olive oil
- 1 leek, sliced
- 3 cloves black garlic, mashed
- 3 cups mixed mushrooms, sliced
- 1 tsp fresh rosemary, chopped
- 2 tbsp flour
- 1 ½ cups vegetable stock
- ¼ cup cream or plant cream
- 1 sheet puff pastry (vegan or regular)
- Salt and pepper to taste

Method

1. Preheat oven to 200°C (390°F).
2. In a skillet, sauté leek in butter/oil until soft. Add mushrooms, cook until golden.
3. Stir in mashed black garlic and rosemary.
4. Sprinkle in flour, stir well, then add stock and cream. Simmer until thick.
5. Spoon mixture into a baking dish. Cover with pastry, seal edges, and cut a small vent.
6. Bake 25–30 minutes until golden.

Black garlic deepens the flavour and magic — inviting protection and transformation at the veil's thinnest.

Dark Ale & Onion Sausages

Ingredients
(Serves 4)

- 1 tbsp oil
- 1 large red onion, thinly sliced
- 1 tbsp brown sugar
- 1 tbsp flour
- ½ cup dark ale (or vegetable stock)
- 4 hearty plant-based or traditional sausages
- 1 tsp mustard
- Salt and pepper

Method

1. Cook sausages as desired (grill, bake, or pan-fry).
2. In a skillet, heat oil and cook onions until soft.
3. Add sugar, cook 2 more minutes, then sprinkle in flour. Stir.
4. Slowly pour in ale, stirring constantly. Simmer until thick.
5. Add mustard, season, and serve warm over sausages.

Dark ale draws on the deep roots of the season — a tribute to ancestors and the underworld's mysteries.

Roast Pumpkin & Chestnut Bake

Ingredients
(Serves 4)

- 2 tbsp olive oil
- 3 cups pumpkin, cubed
- 1 cup cooked chestnuts, halved
- 1 red onion, sliced
- 1 tsp ground cinnamon
- ½ tsp nutmeg
- 1 tbsp maple syrup
- Salt and pepper to taste
- Fresh sage leaves

Method

1. Preheat oven to 200°C (390°F).
2. Toss pumpkin, chestnuts, and onion with oil, spices, syrup, salt, and pepper.
3. Spread on a baking tray and roast 30–35 minutes, stirring once.
4. Serve with crisped sage leaves on top.

Pumpkin and chestnuts offer nourishment and balance — ideal for feasting, reflection, and release.

Root & Barley Stew

Ingredients
(Serves 4–6)

- 1 tbsp olive oil
- 1 large onion, diced
- 2 cloves garlic, minced
- 2 carrots, chopped
- 2 parsnips, chopped
- 2 potatoes, chopped
- 1 cup diced turnip or rutabaga
- ¾ cup pearl barley
- 6 cups vegetable broth
- 2 tsp dried thyme
- 1 tsp smoked paprika
- Salt and pepper to taste
- Fresh parsley, to serve

Method

1. Heat oil in a large pot. Sauté onion and garlic until soft.
2. Add all root vegetables and cook for 5 minutes, stirring.
3. Stir in barley, broth, thyme, paprika, salt, and pepper.
4. Bring to a boil, then reduce heat and simmer for 45–50 minutes, until barley is tender.
5. Serve hot, garnished with parsley.

This earthy stew grounds and warms — perfect for honouring the ancestors and welcoming winter's chill.

Samhain Shepherd's Pie

Ingredients
(Serves 4–6)

- 1 tbsp olive oil
- 1 onion, chopped
- 2 garlic cloves, minced
- 2 carrots, diced
- 1 cup lentils (brown or green), cooked
- 1 tbsp tomato paste
- 1 tsp smoked paprika
- 1 tsp thyme
- 1 cup vegetable broth
- 3–4 cups mashed potatoes
- Optional: grated cheese for topping

Method

1. Heat oil in a skillet, sauté onion and garlic until fragrant.
2. Add carrots, cooked lentils, tomato paste, and spices. Stir.
3. Pour in broth and simmer until thickened, 10–15 minutes.
4. Transfer to a baking dish. Spread mashed potatoes over top.
5. Bake at 200°C (390°F) for 20–25 minutes, until golden. Add cheese in final 10 minutes if using.

Layered and comforting, this dish speaks of cycles — the end of one harvest, the promise of rest.

Amber Sugar Skulls

Ingredients
(Makes about 6–8 small molded skulls)

- 1 cup light brown sugar
- 1 tbsp maple syrup or golden syrup
- 1 tsp water
- Optional: edible gold dust or orange food shimmer

Method

1. In a bowl, mix sugar, syrup, and water until it feels like damp sand. Add a few more drops of water if needed — it should hold its shape when squeezed.
2. Press firmly into small skull molds (silicone works best).
3. Allow to air dry for 24 hours or bake at 150°C (300°F) for 10–12 minutes until hardened.
4. Cool completely before removing.
5. Dust with edible shimmer if desired.

Place on your ancestor altar, use as edible decor, or stir into coffee or tea. These sweet offerings honor the spirits with love and beauty.

Ancestor's Baked Apples

Ingredients
(Serves 4)

- 4 large apples, cored
- ¼ cup raisins or chopped dates
- ¼ cup chopped walnuts or pecans
- 2 tbsp brown sugar or maple syrup
- ½ tsp cinnamon
- Pinch of ground clove
- Butter or dairy-free margarine

A humble, sacred offering — apples are the fruit of the Otherworld and wisdom beyond the veil.

Method

1. Preheat oven to 180°C (350°F).
2. Mix dried fruit, nuts, sugar, and spices.
3. Stuff each apple with filling, top with a small knob of butter.
4. Place in a baking dish with ½ cup water.
5. Bake 30–40 minutes until apples are soft but not collapsed.

Candied Rosemary Pears

Ingredients
(Serves 4)

- 4 ripe but firm pears, halved and cored
- ¼ cup honey or maple syrup
- 1 tbsp lemon juice
- 2 sprigs fresh rosemary
- ¼ tsp cinnamon
- Pinch of salt

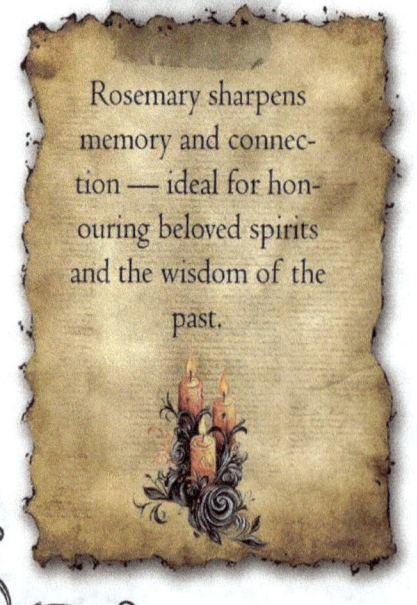

Rosemary sharpens memory and connection — ideal for honouring beloved spirits and the wisdom of the past.

Method

1. Preheat oven to 180°C (350°F).
2. Arrange pear halves in a baking dish, cut side up.
3. In a small pan, warm honey/maple syrup with lemon juice, rosemary, cinnamon, and salt. Simmer 2 minutes.
4. Drizzle syrup over pears.
5. Bake for 25–30 minutes, basting halfway through, until tender and caramelised.
6. Serve warm with cream or yoghurt.

Soulfire Fudge

Ingredients
(Makes one 8x8" pan)

- 3 cups sugar
- ¾ cup butter
- 2/3 cup evaporated milk
- 2 cups chocolate chips
- 1 jar (7 oz) marshmallow crème
- 1 tsp vanilla extract
- Pinch of sea salt
- Optional: chopped dried cherries or toasted nuts

This rich fudge carries warmth and sweetness into the long night — a treat for both living and spirit guests.

Method

1. In a saucepan, combine sugar, butter, and milk. Bring to boil, stirring constantly.
2. Boil 4–5 minutes, stirring. Remove from heat.
3. Stir in chocolate chips, marshmallow crème, vanilla, and salt.
4. Fold in extras if using.
5. Pour into a lined pan, cool completely.
6. Cut into squares and store airtight.

Spirit-Walk Truffles

Ingredients
(Makes ~12 truffles)

- 200g dark chocolate (at least 70%), chopped
- ½ cup heavy cream or coconut cream
- 1 tbsp brandy or strong coffee (optional)
- Pinch of cayenne pepper
- Cocoa powder, crushed nuts, or dried rose petals for rolling

Method

1. Gently heat cream until steaming. Remove from heat, add chocolate. Let sit 2 mins.
2. Stir until smooth. Add brandy/coffee and cayenne.
3. Chill 1 hour, or until firm enough to shape.
4. Roll into balls and coat in toppings of choice.
5. Store chilled.

Dark, rich, and gently spiced — these truffles are perfect for divination nights and dreamwork meditations.

Witchlight Treacle Tart

Ingredients
(Serves 6–8)

- 1 shortcrust pie shell (homemade or pre-made)
- 1 cup golden syrup (or light treacle)
- 2 cups fresh breadcrumbs
- Zest of 1 lemon
- 2 tbsp lemon juice
- 1 egg, beaten

Method

1. Preheat oven to 190°C (375°F).
2. In a bowl, mix syrup, breadcrumbs, lemon zest, juice, and egg.
3. Pour into pie shell and smooth the top.
4. Bake for 25–30 minutes, until golden and set.
5. Cool slightly before serving.

Sweet and sticky with the golden light of harvest — perfect to brighten a shadowed season.

Ancestor's Mulberry Cordial

Ingredients
(Makes about 2 cups concentrate)

- 2 cups fresh or frozen mulberries
- 1 cup sugar or honey
- ¾ cup water
- 1 tbsp lemon juice
- ½ tsp cardamom (optional)

Method

1. Simmer mulberries, sugar, and water in a pan for 20–25 minutes.
2. Mash and strain through a fine sieve or cloth.
3. Stir in lemon juice and cardamom. Bottle and refrigerate.
4. Mix with still or sparkling water to serve.

Offer a sip to the spirits — mulberries are a fruit of mystery, memory, and gentle power.

Blackberry & Elder Syrup

Ingredients
(Makes ~1 cup concentrate)

- 1 cup fresh or frozen blackberries
- ½ cup dried elderberries
- 2 cups water
- ½ cup honey
- 1 tsp grated fresh ginger

Method

1. Simmer berries, water, and ginger for 30 minutes.
2. Strain through muslin or fine sieve.
3. Stir in honey while warm, bottle, and refrigerate.

Take a spoonful daily for protection and immunity. Ideal for winter's edge — and ancestral offerings.

Blood Moon Beetroot Latte

Ingredients
(Serves 1–2)

- 1 small cooked beetroot, puréed
- 1 cup milk of choice
- ½ tsp cinnamon
- ½ tsp ginger
- 1 tsp honey or maple syrup
- Optional: shot of espresso or pinch of cayenne

Method

1. Blend beet purée with milk, spices, and sweetener.
2. Heat gently and whisk until frothy.
3. Serve warm in a deep mug.

Beetroot carries deep, grounding energy — ideal for rooting your spirit while honouring the thinning veil.

Ghost Milk Moon Elixir

Ingredients
(Serves 2)

- 2 cups almond or oat milk
- 1 tsp vanilla extract
- ½ tsp cinnamon
- ¼ tsp nutmeg
- 1 tbsp maple syrup
- Optional: pinch of ashwagandha or reishi powder

Drink before bed for dreamwork or spirit connection — warm, spiced milk is a balm for the soul.

Method

1. Gently warm milk in a saucepan with all other ingredients.
2. Whisk until steamy and frothy.
3. Pour into mugs and sip slowly under the moonlight.

Mulled Blackberry Wine

Ingredients
(Serves 4–6)

- 1 bottle red wine (750ml)
- 1 cup blackberry juice or purée
- ¼ cup honey or sugar (to taste)
- 1 cinnamon stick
- 3 whole cloves
- 2 star anise
- 1 strip orange peel

Method

1. Combine all ingredients in a saucepan.
2. Warm gently over low heat for 15–20 minutes — do not boil.
3. Strain and serve warm in heat-proof cups.

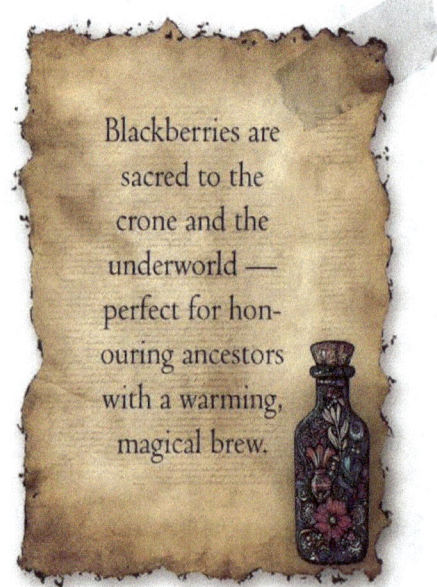

Blackberries are sacred to the crone and the underworld — perfect for honouring ancestors with a warming, magical brew.

Witch's Bonfire Cider

Ingredients
(Serves 4–6)

- 4 cups apple cider (non-alcoholic or hard)
- 1 orange, sliced
- 1 cinnamon stick
- 3 slices fresh ginger
- 4 allspice berries
- 1–2 tbsp brown sugar or maple syrup

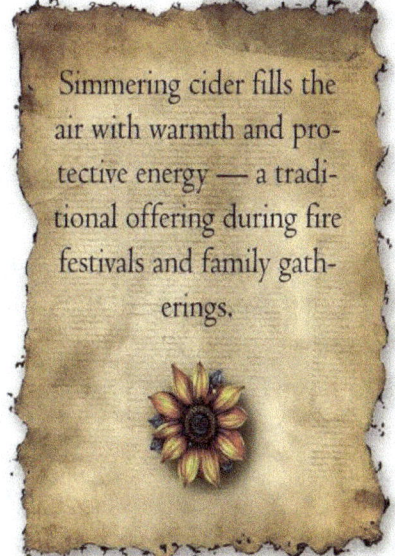

Simmering cider fills the air with warmth and protective energy — a traditional offering during fire festivals and family gatherings.

Method

1. Combine all ingredients in a pot.
2. Simmer gently for 15–20 minutes.
3. Serve hot in mugs, garnished with orange slices.

Caramelised Onion & Fig Relish

Ingredients
(Makes ~2 small jars)

- 2 large red onions, finely sliced
- 1 tbsp olive oil
- ½ cup chopped dried figs
- ¼ cup balsamic vinegar
- 2 tbsp brown sugar
- 1 tsp thyme (fresh or dried)
- Salt to taste

Serve with cheese or roasted meats during your Samhain feast — figs carry the sweetness of old wisdom

Method

1. Sauté onions in oil over medium-low heat until soft and caramelised (15–20 mins).
2. Stir in figs, vinegar, sugar, thyme, and salt.
3. Simmer another 15 minutes until sticky and thick.
4. Spoon into jars and refrigerate.

Cranberry & Orange Spirit Jam

Ingredients
(Makes ~3 cups)

- 3 cups cranberries (fresh or frozen)
- 1 cup orange juice
- Zest of 1 orange
- 1½ cups sugar
- 1 cinnamon stick

Method

1. Combine all ingredients in a pot and bring to a boil.
2. Reduce to simmer and cook 20–25 minutes until cranberries burst and jam thickens.
3. Remove cinnamon stick, spoon into jars, and seal.

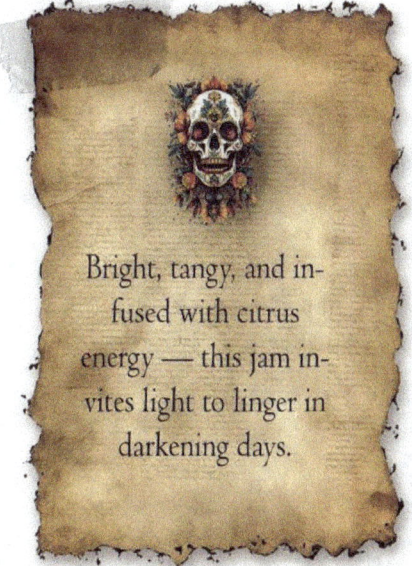

Bright, tangy, and infused with citrus energy — this jam invites light to linger in darkening days.

Mulling Spice Sachets

Ingredients
(Makes 4 sachets, enough for 4 bottles of wine or cider)

- 4 cinnamon sticks
- 2 tbsp whole cloves
- 2 tbsp dried orange peel
- 1 tbsp allspice berries
- 2 star anise pods
- 1 tsp grated nutmeg
- 4 small squares of muslin or cheesecloth
- Kitchen string

Method
1. Break cinnamon sticks into pieces. Mix all spices in a bowl.
2. Divide evenly between the 4 cloth squares.
3. Tie into little bundles with string.
4. Store in an airtight jar or gift in brown paper with instructions.

To use: Simmer with 1 bottle of red wine or 1L cider for 20 minutes. Sweeten to taste.

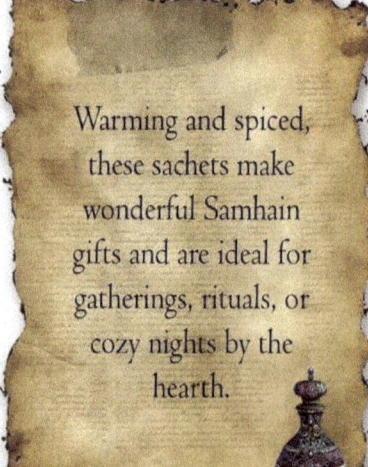

Warming and spiced, these sachets make wonderful Samhain gifts and are ideal for gatherings, rituals, or cozy nights by the hearth.

Smoky Beet & Apple Chutney

Ingredients
(Makes ~2–3 small jars)

- 2 medium beets, peeled and grated
- 2 apples, peeled and chopped
- ½ cup chopped red onion
- ½ cup cider vinegar
- ¼ cup brown sugar
- ½ tsp smoked paprika
- ¼ tsp allspice
- Salt to taste

Method

1. Place all ingredients in a saucepan.
2. Simmer uncovered for 45–60 minutes, stirring occasionally, until thick and glossy.
3. Spoon into sterilised jars and seal.

Rich in earthy energy, this chutney honours root magic and ancestral grounding.

Spiced Pumpkin Butter

Ingredients
(Makes ~2 cups)

- 2 cups pumpkin purée (fresh or canned)
- ½ cup apple cider
- ½ cup brown sugar (adjust to taste)
- 1 tsp ground cinnamon
- ½ tsp ground ginger
- ¼ tsp nutmeg
- Pinch of salt

Method

1. Combine all ingredients in a saucepan.
2. Simmer gently over low heat, stirring often, for 20–30 minutes until thickened.
3. Spoon into sterilised jars and refrigerate. Use within 2 weeks.

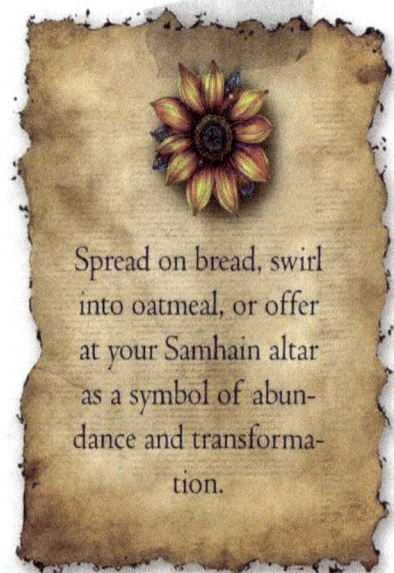

Spread on bread, swirl into oatmeal, or offer at your Samhain altar as a symbol of abundance and transformation.

Ingredients

Method

Notes

"The Earth laughs in flowers."
— Ralph Waldo Emerson

Notes

"Bless the hands that stir with love."
— Traditional

Notes

"Gather the light of the sun, the scent of the herbs, and the hush of the soil — and call it home." — Original

About the Author

With a deep reverence for folklore, plant lore, and the rhythms of the natural world, Morgelyn Hearthwood has spent years exploring the ways food, magic, and seasonal living intertwine. Her debut book, Cauldron and Candlelight, is a celebration of that exploration—offering readers a gentle, nourishing path through the Wheel of the Year, filled with seasonal recipes, sabbat blessings, and heartfelt reflections on kitchen witchcraft.

Morgelyn believes in the magic of the simple and the sacred: hands in the soil, tea brewed with purpose, candles lit with quiet intention. Her writing is infused with warmth and wonder, perfect for anyone seeking to reconnect with the natural world, whether through mindful cooking, herbal wisdom, or personal ritual.

Morgelyn draws creative energy from misty forests, overgrown hedgerows, vintage cookbooks, and the old stories whispered through the leaves.

She writes under the imprint Ember & Ink Books, a name that reflects her love of both storytelling and firelit spaces—places where imagination glows and pages come to life. With each book, she hopes to inspire a return to slowness, intention, and the sacred rhythm of the year.

Whether you are an experienced practitioner, a curious kitchen witch, or simply someone who loves the feel of a good book and a warm hearth, Morgelyn welcomes you to share in her world—one rooted in connection, creativity, and quiet enchantment.

www.ingramcontent.com/pod-product-compliance
Lightning Source LLC
Chambersburg PA
CBHW071231070526
44583CB00017B/2136